Charles H. Master

Canadian Appeals

A Complete Collection of Canadian cases taken on appeal to the Judicial

Committee of the Privy Council

Charles H. Master

Canadian Appeals
A Complete Collection of Canadian cases taken on appeal to the Judicial Committee of the Privy Council

ISBN/EAN: 9783337189426

Printed in Europe, USA, Canada, Australia, Japan

Cover: Foto ©Suzi / pixelio.de

More available books at **www.hansebooks.com**

CANADIAN APPEALS.

A COMPLETE COLLECTION OF CANADIAN CASES

TAKEN ON APPEAL TO THE JUDICIAL COMMITTEE OF THE PRIVY
COUNCIL, AND OF REPORTED CASES CARRIED TO THE
SUPREME COURT OF CANADA, AND THE COURTS OF
APPEAL IN UPPER CANADA AND ONTARIO,
UP TO MARCH 1ST, 1894, SHOWING THE
JUDICIAL HISTORY OF ALL
SUCH CASES.

BY

C. H. MASTERS, B.A.

Barrister;

Assistant Reporter of the Supreme Court of Canada.

TORONTO :

THE CARSWELL Co. (LTD.) LAW PUBLISHERS, ETC.

1894.

TORONTO :
PRINTED BY THE CARSWELL CO. (LTD.)
22, 30 ADELAIDE ST. EAST.

PREFACE.

THIS collection of cases is intended by the compiler to serve as an aid in the study of case law by enabling the lawyer or student examining any reported case to ascertain, by a single reference to the proper list, whether or not such case has been carried to appeal, and if it has what was the result of such appeal and where it is reported. Such being the object of the compilation it is hardly necessary to say that cases reported only on appeal are not inserted, with the exception, however, of those taken to the Privy Council as to which the collection is complete.

To gather together the materials for the preparation of this little volume has called for the expenditure of no small amount of time and labour, and the greatest care has been exercised to insure accuracy. If it proves to be of any value to those engaged in the study and practice of the law, the object of the compilation will have been attained.

C. H. MASTERS.

OTTAWA, April 2nd, 1894.

CONTENTS.

LIST OF ABBREVIATIONS.

[ ] A.C.	Law Reports, Appeal Cases, Present series.
All.	Allen's Reports (New Brunswick).
App. Cas.	Law Reports, Appeal Cases.
A.R.	Ontario Appeal Reports.
Asp. N.S.	Aspinall's Maritime Cases, New series.
B.C.R.	British Columbia Reports.
B.C.L.R.	British Columbia Law Reports.
C.L.J.	Canada Law Journal.
C.P.	Common Pleas Reports (Upper Canada).
Can. Gaz.	Canadian Gazette (Published in London).
Cook V.A.	Cook's Vice-Admiralty Reports (Lower Canada).
Dor. Q.B.	Dorion's Queen's Bench Reports (Lower Canada).
E. & A. Rep.	Error and Appeal Reports (Upper Canada).
Ex. C.R.	Exchequer Court of Canada Reports.
Gr.	Grant's Chancery Reports (Upper Canada).
Jur. N.S.	Jurist, New series (English).
L.C.J.	Lower Canada Jurist.
L.C.L.J.	Lower Canada Law Journal.
L.C.R.	Lower Canada Reports.
L.J.	Law Journal, New series (English).
L.N.	Legal News (Montreal).
L.R.P.C.	Law Reports, Privy Council (English).
L.T.	Law Times, New series (English).
M.L.R.Q.B.	Montreal Law Reports, Queen's Bench.
M.L.R.S.C.	" " " Superior Court.
Man. L.R.	Manitoba Law Reports.
Moo. N.S.	Moore's Privy Council Reports. New series.
Moo. P.C.	" " " "
N.B. Dig.	New Brunswick Digest (Stevens).
N.B. R.	New Brunswick Reports.
N.B. Rep.	" " "
N.S. Rep.	Nova Scotia Reports.
N.W.T. Rep.	North-West Territories Reports.

O.R.	Ontario Reports.
O.S.	King's Bench Reports, Old series (Upper Canada).
Old.	Oldright's Reports (Nova Scotia).
P. & B.	Pugsley & Burbidge's Reports (New Brunswick).
P.E.I. Rep.	Prince Edward Island Reports.
P.R.	Practice Reports (Ontario).
Pugs.	Pugsley's Reports (New Brunswick).
Q.B.	Upper Canada Queen's Bench Reports,
Q.L.R.	Quebec Law Reports.
Q.R.Q.B.	Quebec Reports, Queen's Bench. Present series.
R. & C.	Russell & Chesley's Reports (Nova Scotia).
R. & G.	Russell & Geldert's Reports (Nova Scotia).
R.E.D.	Russell's Equity Reports (Nova Scotia).
R.L.	La Revue Legale (Lower Canada).
Rev. Crit.	La Revue Critique (Lower Canada).
S.C. Dig.	Cassell's Digest Supreme Court Reports (1893)
S.C.R.	Supreme Court of Canada Reports.
Stewart V.A.Rep.	Stewart's Vice-Admiralty Reports (Nova Scotia).
Stu. L.C.R.	Stuart's Lower Canada Reports.
Stu. V.A.	Stuart's Vice-Admiralty Reports (Lower Canada).
Times L.R.	Times Law Reports (English).
U.C.C.P.	Upper Canada Common Pleas Reports.
U.C.L.J.	Upper Canada Law Journal, Old series.
U.C.Q.B.	Upper Canada Queen's Bench Reports.
W.R.	Weekly Reporter (English).

ADDENDA ET CORRIGENDA.

PAGE 2.—To cases from Supreme Court to Privy Council, add: McAllister v. Forsyth (12 S. C. R. 1) 5 R. & G. 151. Nova Scotia Dig. 147. Leave to appeal refused.

Union Bank of Canada v. O'Gara (22 S. C. R. 404). 22 Can. Gaz. 567. Leave to appeal granted; stands for argument.

PAGE 4.—In Archibald v. The Queen, The Queen v. Demers, The Queen v. Farwell, and S. S. Santandarino v. Vanvert, for result of appeal, read: "Judgment affirmed."

In The Queen v. Ship Oscar & Hattie, read: "Judgment reversed." ·

PAGE 5.—In "Act respecting Assignments and Preferences." for result of appeal, read: "Judgment reversed; and for report on appeal, read: "22 Can. Gaz. 514."

In Tennant v. Union Bank, for report on appeal, read: "[1894] A. C. 31."

PAGE 6.—In Beaver v. G. T. Ry. Co., for result of appeal, read: "Judgment reversed."

PAGE 8.—To Cases from Ontario Courts to Supreme Court, add: Holiday v. Hogan (20 A. R. 298) 22 O. R. 235. 22 S. C. R.. Judgment reversed.

PAGE 11.—In Purcell v. Bergin, for result of appeal; read: "Judgment reversed."

PAGE 12.—In Virgo v. City of Toronto, for result of appeal, read: "Judgment reversed in part."

CASES IN THE SUPREME COURT OF CANADA CARRIED TO THE PRIVY COUNCIL.

CASE.	REPORT ON APPEAL.	RESULT OF APPEAL.
Alexander v. Vye (16 S. C. R. 501) 28 N. B. R. 89.	None.	Leave to appeal refused.
Arpin v. The Queen (14 S. C. R. 736).	10 Can. Gaz. 275.	Leave to appeal refused.
Atty.-Gen. of British Columbia v. Atty.-Gen. of Canada (14 S. C. R. 345).	14 App. Cas. 295; 58 L. J. 88; 60 L. T. 712; 5 Times L. R. 385.	Judgment reversed.
Atty.-Gen. of Canada v. City of Toronto, (S. C. Dig. 57) 18 A. R. 622; 20 O. R. 19.	21 Can. Gaz. 414.	Leave to appeal refused.
Barrett v. City of Winnipeg (19 S. C. R. 374) 7 Man. L. R. 273	[1892] A. C. 445; 61 L.	Judgment reversed.
Beatty v. North West Trans. Co. (12 S. C. R. 598) 11 A. R. 205; 6 O. R. 300.	12 App. Cas. 589; 56 L. J. 102; 57 L. T. 420; 36 W. R. 647.	Judgment reversed.
Beaudet v. North Shore Ry. Co. (15 S. C. R. 44).	10 Can. Gaz. 463.	Leave to appeal refused.
Bickford v. Corporation of Chatham (16 S. C. R. 235) 14 A. R. 32; 10 O. R. 257.	14 Can. Gaz. 153.	Leave to appeal refused.
Canada Atlantic Ry. Co. v. City of Ottawa (12 S. C. R. 365) 12 A. R. 234 (8 O. R. 183, 201). Canada Atlantic Ry. Co. v. Township of Cambridge (15 S. C. R. 219) 14 A. R. 299.	11 Can. Gaz. 394.	Leave to appeal granted in both cases, but appeals not prosecuted.
Canada Central Ry. Co. v. Murray (8 S. C. R. 313) 7 A. R. 646.	8 App. Cas. 574.	Leave to appeal refused.
Canadian Pacific Ry. Co. v. Robinson (19 S. C. R. 292); M. L. R. 6 Q. B. 118; 5 S. C. 225.	[1892] A. C. 481; 61 L. J. 79; 67 L. T. 505.	Judgment reversed.
Central Vermont Ry. Co. v. Town of St. Johns (14 S. C. R. 288) 30 L. C. J. 122.	14 App. Cas. 590; 59 L. J. 15; 61 L. T. 441.	Judgment affirmed.
Chevrier v. The Queen (4 S. C. R. 1).		Leave to appeal refused.
Citizens' Ins. Co. v. Parsons. Queen's Ins. Co. v. Parsons (4 S. C. R. 215) 4 A. R. 96, 103; 43 U. C. Q. B. 261. 271.	7 App. Cas. 96; 51 L. J. 11; 45 L. T. 721.	Judgment affirmed as to validity of Ont. Insurance Act, otherwise reversed.
Duggan v. London & Canadian Loan Co. (20 S. C. R. 481) 18 A. R. 305; 19 O. R. 272.	[1893] A. C. 506; 63 L. J. 14.	Judgment reversed.
Dumoulin v. Langtry (13 S. C. R. 258) 7 O. R. 499, 644.	57 L. T. 317.	Leave to appeal refused.
Dupuy v. Ducondu (6 S. C. R. 425).	9 App. Cas. 150; 53 L. J. 12; 50 L. T. 129.	Judgment reversed.
Exchange Bank of Canada v. La Banque du Peuple (S. C. Dig. 79).	9 Can. Gaz. 394.	Leave to appeal refused.
Forsyth v. Bury (15 S. C. R. 543).	11 Can. Gaz. 413.	Leave to appeal refused.

CASE.	REPORT ON APPEAL.	RESULT OF APPEAL.
Fredericton, City of, v. The Queen (3 S. C. R. 505) 3 P. & B. 139.	Russell v. The Queen, 7 App. Cas. 829.	Judgment affirmed in a case from New Bruns. raising same question.
Gagnon v. Prince (7 S. C. R. 386) 2 Dor. Q. B. 71.	8 App. Cas. 103.	Leave to appeal refused.
Glengarry Election Case (14 S. C. R. 453).	59 L. T. 279; 4 Times L. R. 664.	Leave to appeal refused.
Grand Trunk Ry. Co. v. Beckett (16 S. C. R. 713) 13 A. R. 174; 8 O. R. 601.	9 Can. Gaz. 394.	Leave to appeal refused.
Grand Trunk Ry. Co. v. McMillan (16 S. C. R. 543) 15 A. R. 14; 12 O. R. 103.	Wheeler, P. C. Law 982.	Leave to appeal refused.
Great Western Ins. Co. v. Jordan (14 S. C. R. 734) 24 N. B. R. 421.	8 Can. Gaz. 464.	Leave to appeal granted but appeal never prosecuted.
Halifax & Cape Breton Coal and Ry. Co. v. Gregory (S. C. Dig. 727) 4 R. & G. 436.	11 App. Cas. 229; 55 L. J. 40; 55 L. T. 270; *sub nom.* Atty.-Gen of Nova Scotia v. Gregory.	Leave to appeal refused.
Hoggan v. Esquimault & Nanaimo Ry. Co. (20 S. C. R. 235).	None.	Stands for argument.
Johnson v. Trustees of St. Andrew's Church (1 S. C. R. 235) 18 L. C. J. 113; 5 R. L. 48.	3 App. Cas. 159; 37 L. T. 556; 26 W. R. 359.	Leave to appeal refused.
Kearney v. Creelman (14 S. C. R. 33) 6 R. & G. 92.	8 Can. Gaz. 154.	Leave to appeal refused.
Lamoureux v. Molleur (S. C. Dig. 71).	8 Can. Gaz. 154.	Leave to appeal refused.
Lawless v. Sullivan (3 S. C. R. 117) 1 P. & B. 431.	6 App. Cas. 373; 50 L. J. 33; 44 L. T. 897; 29 W. R. 917.	Judgment reversed.
Les Ecclesiastiques de St. Sulpice v. City of Montreal (16 S. C. R. 399) M. L. R. 4 Q. B. 1; 2 S. C. 265.	14 App. Cas. 660; 59 L. J. 20; 61 L. T. 653.	Leave to appeal refused.
Lewin v. Wilson (9 S. C. R. 637).	11 App. Cas. 639; 55 L. J. 75; 55 L. T. 410; 2 Times L. R. 741.	Judgment reversed.
Liquor License Act, 1883, *In re*, (S. C. Dig. 509).	6 Can Gaz. 152, 265.	Judgment holding Act valid as to wholesale licenses reversed.
Maritime Bank v. The Queen (17 S. C. R. 657) 27 N. B. R. 357.	15 Can. Gaz. 394.	Leave to appeal refused.
Maritime Bank v. Rec.-Gen. of New Brunswick (20 S. C. R. 695) 27 N. B. R. 379.	[1892] A. C. 437; 61 L. J. 75; 67 L. T. 126.	Judgment affirmed.
Martley v. Carson (20 S. C. R. 634).	14 Can. Gaz. 270, *sub nom.* Clark v. Carson.	Appeal dismissed on preliminary objections, merits not decided.
Mercer v. The Atty.-Gen. of Ontario (5 S. C. R. 538) 6 A. R. 576; 26 Gr. 126.	8 App. Cas. 767; 52 L. J. 84; 49 L. T. 312.	Judgment reversed.
Moffatt v. Merchants' Bank of Canada (11 S. C. R. 46) 5 O. R. 122.	6 Can. Gaz. 153.	Leave to appeal refused.
Moore v. Connecticut Mutual Ins. Co. (6 S. C. R. 634) 3 A. R. 230; 41 U. C. Q. B. 497.	6 App. Cas. 644.	Judgment affirmed.
McLaren v. Caldwell (8 S. C. R. 435) 5 A. R. 363.	9 App. Cas. 392; 53 L. J. 33; 51 L. T. 370.	Judgment reversed.
McQueen v. The Queen (16 S. C. R. 1).	11 Can. Gaz. 368.	Leave to appeal refused.
Nasmith v. Manning (5 S. C. R. 417) 5 A. R. 126; 29 C. P. 34.	None.	Leave to appeal granted, but appeal not prosecuted.

CASE.	REPORT ON APPEAL.	RESULT OF APPEAL.
Parker v. Montreal City Passenger Ry. Co. (S. C. Dig. 731) 7 L. N. 194.	6 Can. Gaz. 174.	Leave to appeal refused.
Pion v. North Shore Ry. Co. (14 S. C. R. 674) 12 Q. L. R. 205.	14 App. Cas. 612; 59 L. J. 25; 61 L. T. 525.	Judgment affirmed.
Pontiac, County of, v. Ross (17 S. C. R. 406).	None.	Leave to appeal refused.
Quebec, City of, v. Quebec Central Ry. Co. (10 S. C. R. 563).	None.	Leave to appeal granted, but appeal not prosecuted.
Queen, The, v. Belleau (7 S. C. R. 53).	7 App. Cas. 473.	Judgment reversed.
Queen, The, v. Doutre (6 S. C. R. 342).	9 App. Cas. 745; 53 L. J. 85; 51 L. T. 669.	Judgment affirmed.
Reed v. Mousseau (Atty.-Gen. of Quebec (8 S. C. R. 408) 26 L. C. J. 331.	10 App. Cas. 141; 54 L. J. 12; 52 L. T. 393; 33 W. R. 618, *sub nom.* Atty.-Gen. of Quebec v. Reed.	Judgment affirmed.
Ross v. Hurteau (18 S. C. R. 713).	None.	Leave to appeal refused.
Russell v. Lefrançois (8 S. C. R. 335) 2 Dor. Q. B. 245.	None.	Leave to appeal refused.
Sewell v. British Columbia Towing Co. (9 S. C. R. 527).	None.	Leave to appeal granted, but appeal never prosecuted.
Shields v. Leacock (S. C. Dig. 604).	None.	Leave to appeal granted, but appeal not prosecuted.
Smith v. Goldie (9 S. C. R. 46) 7 A. R. 628	None.	Leave to appeal refused.
St. Catharines Milling Co. v. The Queen (13 S. C. R. 577) 13 A. R. 148; 10 O. R. 196.	14 App. Cas. 46; 58 L. J. 54; 60 L. T. 197; 5 Times L. R. 125.	Judgment affirmed.
St. Lawrence & Ottawa Ry. Co. v. Lett (11 S. C. R. 422) 11 A. R. 1; 1 O. R. 545.	6 Can. Gaz. 583.	Leave to appeal refused.
Sweeny v. Bank of Montreal (12 S. C. R. 661) 5 L. N. 66.	12 App. Cas. 617; 56 L. J. 79; 56 L. T. 897.	Judgment affirmed.
Valin v. Langlois (3 S. C. R. 1) 5 Q. L. R. 1.	5 App. Cas. 115; 49 L. J. 37; 41 L. T. 662.	Leave to appeal refused.
Wadsworth v. McCord (12 S. C. R. 466) M. L. R. 2 Q. B. 113.	14 App. Cas. 631; 59 L. J. 7; 61 L. T. 487, *sub nom.* McMullen v. Wadsworth.	Judgment affirmed.
West v. Corporation of Parkdale (12 S. C. R. 250) 12 A. R. 393; 8 O. R. 59; 7 O. R. 276.	12 App. Cas. 602; 56 L. J. 66; 57 L. T. 602.	Judgment affirmed.
Williams v. Township of Raleigh (21 S. C. R. 103).	[1893] A. C. 540, 63 L. J. 1; 69 L. T. 506.	Judgment reversed.
Windsor & Annapolis Ry. Co. v. The Queen (10 S. C. R. 335).	55 L. J. 41; 55 L. T. 274; 2 Times L. R. 743.	Judgment as to *quantum* of damages reversed.

CASES IN THE EXCHEQUER COURT OF CANADA CARRIED TO THE SUPREME COURT.

CASE.	REPORT ON APPEAL.	RESULT OF APPEAL.
Archibald v. The Queen (3 Ex. C. R. 251).	———	Stands for judgment.
Atty.-Gen. of Ontario v. Atty.-Gen. of Canada (1 Ex. C. R. 184).	14 S. C. R. 736.	Judgment affirmed.
Bulmer v. The Queen (3 Ex. C. R. 184).	———	Stands for judgment.
Burroughs v. The Queen (2 Ex. C. R. 293).	20 S. C. R. 420.	Judgment affirmed.
Carter v. Hamilton (3 Ex. C. R. 351).	———	Stands for argument.
Carter, Macy & Co. v. The Queen (2 Ex. C. R. 126).	18 S. C. R. 706.	Judgment affirmed.
Charland v. The Queen (1 Ex. C. R. 291).	16 S. C. R. 721.	Judgment affirmed.
Clarke v. The Queen (2 Ex. C. R. 141; 3 Ex. C. R. 1).	21 S. C. R. 656.	Leave to appeal refused as to questions reported in Exchequer Court.
Guay v. The Queen (2 Ex. C. R. 18).	17 S. C. R. 30.	Judgment reversed.
Humphreys v. The Queen (2 Ex. C. R. 386).	20 S. C. R. 591.	Judgment affirmed.
Kearney v. The Queen (2 Ex. C. R. 21).	S. C. Dig. 313.	Judgment reversed as to measure of damages.
Martin v. The Queen (2 Ex. C. R. 328).	20 S. C. R. 240.	Judgment reversed.
Mayes v. The Queen (2 Ex. C. R. 403).	———	Stands for argument.
Merchants Bank of Canada v. The Queen (1 Ex. C. R. 1).	S. C. Dig. 636.	Judgment reversed.
Morin v. The Queen (2 Ex. C. R. 396).	20 S. C. R. 515.	Judgment affirmed.
McGreevy v. The Queen (1 Ex. C. R. 321).	18 S. C. R. 371.	Judgment reversed.
Paint v. The Queen (2 Ex. C. R. 149).	18 S. C. R. 718.	Judgment affirmed.
Paradis v. The Queen (1 Ex. C. R. 191).	16 S. C. R. 716.	Judgment reversed.
Queen, The, v. Demers (3 Ex. C. R. 293).	———	Stands for judgment.
Queen, The, v. Farwell (3 Ex. C. R. 271).	———	Stands for judgment.
Queen, The, v. Ship Oscar and Hattie (3 Ex. C. R. 241).	———	Stands for judgment.
Queen, The, v. St. John Water Commissioners, (2 Ex. C. R. 78).	19 S. C. R. 125.	Judgment affirmed.
S. S. Santandarino v. Vanvert (3 Ex. C. R. 378).	———	Stands for judgment.
Ship Quebec in re (3 Ex. C. R. 33).	20 S. C. R. 472.	Judgment affirmed.
Starrs v. The Queen (1 Ex. C. R. 301).	17 S. C. R. 118.	Judgment reversed.
Vezina v. The Queen (2 Ex. C. R. 11).	17 S. C. R. 1.	Judgment reversed.

CASES IN THE ONTARIO COURTS CARRIED TO THE PRIVY COUNCIL.

CASE.	REPORT ON APPEAL.	RESULT OF APPEAL.
Act respecting Assignments and Preferences (20 A. R. 489).	22 Can. Gaz. 274.	Stands for judgment.
Baldwin v. Kingstone (18 A. R. 63) 16 O. R. 341.	17 Can. Gaz. 400	Re-argument ordered by Jud. Com. which was not proceeded with.
Bowes v. City of Toronto (6 Gr. 1) 4 Gr. 489.	11 Moo. P. C. 463.	Judgment affirmed.
Cameron v. Bickford (11 A. R. 52).	6 Can. Gaz. 514.	Judgment reversed.
Canada Central Ry. Co. v. McLaren (8 A. R. 564) 32 C. P. 324.	3 Can. Gaz. 321, 346.	Judgment affirmed.
Counter v. Macpherson (N. R.)	5 Moo. P. C. 83.	Judgment affirmed.
De Souza, in re. (9 O. R. 39).	1 Times L. R. 597.	Leave to appeal refused.
Gilmour v. Supple, 5 C. P. 318.	11 Moo. P. C. 551; 6 W. R. 445.	Judgment affirmed.
Grand Junction Ry. Co. v. County of Peterboro' (13 A. R. 420).	13 App. Cas. 136.	Judgment affirmed.
Great Western Ry. Co. v. Braid. Great Western Ry. Co. v. Fawcett (7 U. C. L. J. 43).	1 Moo. N. S. 101; 9 Jur. N. S. 339; 8 L. T. 31; 11 W. R. 444.	Judgment affirmed.
Great Western Ry. Co. v. Commercial Bank of Canada (2 E. & A. 285) 22 Q. B. 233.	3 Moo. N. S. 295; 13 L. T. 105.	Judgment affirmed.
Greenshields v. Barnhart (3 Gr. 1) 1 Gr. 459.	9 Moo. P. C. 18; 5 Gr. 99.	Judgment affirmed.
Huntington v. Attrill (18 A. R. 136) 17 O. R. 245.	[1893] A. C. 150; 62 L. J. 44.	Judgment reversed.
International Bridge Co. v. Canada Southern Ry. Co. (7 A. R. 226).	8 App. Cas. 723.	Judgment affirmed.
Jennings v. Grand Trunk Ry. Co. (15 A. R. 477).	13 App. Cas. 800; 58 L. J. 1; 59 L. T. 679; 37 W. R. 403; 4 Times L. R. 752.	Judgment affirmed.
Lindsay Petroleum Oil Co. v. Hurd (17 Gr. 115) 16 Gr. 147.	L. R. 5 P. C. 221; 22 W. R. 492.	Judgment reversed.
Matthews v. Holmes (5 Gr. 1) 3 Gr. 379.	9 Moo. P. C. 413; 5 Gr. 108.	Judgment affirmed.
Oliver, in re.	11 Can. Gaz. 294.	Leave to appeal refused.
Peart v. Grand Trunk Ry. Co. (10 A. R. 191).	6 Can. Gaz. 535.	Judgment affirmed.
Powell v. Washburn (N. R.)	2 Moo. P. C. 199.	Judgment affirmed.
Ratte v. Booth (14 A. R. 419) 11 O. R. 491; 10 O. R. 351.	15 App. Cas. 188; 59 L. J. 41; 62 L. T. 198; 38 W. R. 737.	Judgment affirmed.
Reg. v. Hodge (7 A. R. 246) 46 Q. B. 141.	9 App. Cas. 117; 53 L. J. 1; 50 L. T. 301.	Judgment affirmed.
Simpson v. Smythe (1 E. & A. 1,172; 2 O. S. 1,129).	7 Moo. P. C. 205.	Judgment affirmed.
Smart v. Smart	[1892] A. C. 425; 61 L. J. 38; 67 L. T. 198.	Judgment affirmed.
Tennant v. Union Bank (19 A. R. 1).	22 Can. Gaz. 256.	Judgment affirmed.
Toronto, City of, and Toronto Street Ry. Co. in re (20 A. R. 125) 22 O. R. 374.	[1893] A. C. 511.	Judgment affirmed.

CASES IN THE ONTARIO COURTS CARRIED TO THE SUPREME COURT OF CANADA.

CASE.	REPORT ON APPEAL.	RESULT OF APPEAL.
Abell v. Church 26 C. P. 338.	1 S. C. R. 442.	Judgment reversed.
Adamson v. Adamson (7 A. R. 592) 28 Gr. 226.	12 S. C. R. 563.	Judgment affirmed.
Archer v. Severn (8 A. R. 725).	S. C. Dig. 875.	Judgment reversed.
Atty.-Gen. of Canada v. City of Toronto (18 A. R. 622) 20 O. R. 19.	S. C. Dig. 57.	Judgment reversed, and leave to appeal to Privy Council refused.
Atty.-Gen. of Ontario v. O'Reilly (6 A. R. 576) 26 Gr. 126.	5 S. C. R. 538 sub nom. Mercer v. Atty.-Gen. of Ontario.	Judgment reversed, but restored on further appeal, 8 App. Cas. 767.
Atty.-Gen. v. Vaughan Road Co. 19 A. R. 234 ; 21 O. R. 507.	21 S. C. R. 631.	Judgment reversed.
Badenach v. Slater (8 A. R. 402).	10 S. C. R. 296.	Judgment affirmed.
Ball v. Crompton Corset Co. (12 A. R. 738) 9 O. R. 228.	13 S. C. R. 469.	Judgment affirmed.
Bank of Montreal v. Haffner. Bank of Montreal v. Worswick (10 A. R. 592) 3 O. R. 183.	S. C. Dig. 526.	Judgment affirmed.
Barned's Banking Co. v. Reynolds (3 A. R. 371) 36 Q. B. 256 ; 40 Q. B. 435.	S. C. Dig. 170.	Judgment reversed.
Barton, Township of, v. City of Hamilton (17 A. R. 346) 18 O. R. 199.	20 S. C. R. 173.	Judgment affirmed.
Bate v. Canadian Pacific Ry. Co. (15 A. R. 388) 14 O. R. 625.	18 S. C. R. 697.	Judgment reversed.
Beatty v. Neelon (12 A. R. 50) 9 O. R 385.	13 S. C. R. 1.	Judgment affirmed.
Beatty v. North-West Importation Co. (11 A. R. 205) 6 O. R. 300.	12 S. C. R. 598.	Judgment reversed, but restored on further appeal. 12 App. Cas. 589.
Beaver v. Grand Trunk Ry. Co. (20 A. R. 476) 22 O. R. 167.	———	Stands for judgment.
Beckett v. Grand Trunk Ry. Co. (13 A. R. 174) 8 O. R. 601.	16 S. C. R. 713.	Judgment affirmed, and leave to appeal to Privy Council refused.
Bell v. Fraser (12 A. R. 1).	13 S. C. R. 546.	Judgment affirmed.
Bell v. Macklin (23 C. L. J. 299).	15 S. C. R. 576.	Judgment affirmed.
Bickford v. Town of Chatham (14 A. R. 32) 10 O. R. 257.	16 S. C. R. 235.	Judgment affirmed.
Billington v. Provincial Ins. Co. (2 A. R. 158) 24 Gr. 299.	3 S. C. R. 182.	Judgment affirmed.
Birkett v. McGuire (7 A. R. 53) 31 C. P. 430.	S. C. Dig. 598.	Judgment reversed.
Brantford, &c., Ry. Co. v. Huffman (18 A. R. 415).	19 S. C. R. 336.	Judgment affirmed.
Brown v. Great Western Ry. Co. (2 A. R. 64) 40 Q. B. 333.	3 S. C. R. 259.	Judgment affirmed.

CASE.	REPORT ON APPEAL.	RESULT OF APPEAL.
Bull v. Imperial Ins. Co. (15 A. R. 421) 14 O. R. 322.	18 S. C. R. 697.	Judgment affirmed.
Cameron v. Wait (3 A. R. 175) 27 C. P. 475.	S. C. Dig. 332.	Judgment affirmed.
Campbell v. Kingston & Bath Road Co. (18 A. R. 286).	20 S. C. R. 605.	Judgment affirmed.
Campbell v. McDougall (5 A. R. 503) 26 Gr. 280.	6 S. C. R. 502.	Judgment affirmed.
Campbell v. Roche. McKinnon v. Roche (18 A. R. 646).	21 S. C. R. 645 *sub nom.* Campbell v. Patterson and Mader v. McKinnon.	Judgment affirmed.
Canada Atlantic Ry. Co. v. City of Ottawa (12 A. R. 234) 8 O. R. 183, 201.	12 S. C. R. 365.	Judgment affirmed. Leave granted to appeal to Pr. Coun., but not proceeded with.
Canada Atlantic Ry. Co. v. Township of Cambridge (14 A. R. 299) 11 O. R. 392.	15 S. C. R. 219.	Judgment affirmed. Leave to appeal to Pr. Coun. granted, but not proceeded with.
Cannon, *in re* Oates v. Cannon, 13 O. R. 70, 705.	S. C. Dig. 111.	Judgment affirmed.
Carey v. City of Toronto (11 A. R. 416) 7 O. R. 195.	14 S. C. R. 172.	Judgment affirmed.
Church v. Fenton (4 A. R. 159) 28 C. P. 384.	5 S. C. R. 239.	Judgment affirmed.
Citizen's Ins. Co. and Henderson *in re* (13 P. R. 70).	18 S. C. R. 338 *sub nom.* Green v. Citizens' Ins. Co.	Judgment affirmed.
Clarke & Union Fire Ins. Co. *in re* (16 A. R. 161) 10 O. R. 489 ; 13 A. R. 268 ; 14 S. C. R. 624.	17 S. C. R. 265 *sub nom.* Shoolbred v. Clarke.	Judgment affirmed.
Clouse v. Canada Southern Ry. Co. (11 A. R. 287) 4 O. R. 28.	13 S. C. R. 139.	Judgment reversed.
Conmee v. Bond (16 A. R. 398) 15 O. R. 716.	S. C. Dig. 511.	Judgment affirmed.
Connell v. Town of Prescott (20 A. R. 49).	22 S. C. R. 147.	Judgment affirmed.
Cosgrave v. Boyle (5 A. R. 458) 45 Q. B. 32.	6 S. C. R. 165.	Judgment reversed.
Cosgrave Brewing & Malting Co. v. Starrs (11 A. R. 156) 5 O. R. 189.	12 S. C. R. 571.	Judgment reversed.
Crysler v. McKay (2 A. R. 569).	3 S. C. R. 436.	Judgment reversed.
Cumming v. Landed Banking & Loan Co. (19 A. R. 447) 20 O. R. 382 ; 19 O. R. 426.	22 S. C. R. 246.	Judgment reversed.
Curry v. Curry (4 A. R. 63) 26 Gr. 1.	S. C. Dig. 778.	Judgment affirmed by equal division.
Davidson v. Oliver (6 A. R. 595).	11 S. C. R. 166.	Judgment reversed.
Dillon v. Township of Raleigh (13 A. R. 53).	14 S. C. R. 739.	Judgment affirmed.
Dixon v. Richelieu Navigation Co. (15 A. R. 647)	18 S. C. R. 704.	Judgment affirmed.
Donovan v. Herbert (12 A. R. 298) 9 O. R. 89.	S. C. Dig. 653.	Judgment affirmed.
Dorland v. Jones (12 A. R. 543) 7 O. R. 17.	14 S. C. R. 39.	Judgment affirmed.
Dover, Township of, v. Town of Chatham (11 A. R. 248) 5 O. R. 325.	12 S. C. R. 321.	Judgment affirmed.
Duggan v. London & Canadian Loan Co. (18 A. R. 305) 19 O. R. 272.	20 S. C. R. 481, reversed by P.C. [1893] A.C. 506	Judgment reversed, but restored on further app.

CASE.	REPORT ON APPEAL.	RESULT OF APPEAL.
Duncan v. Rogers (16 A. R. 3) 15 O. R. 699.	18 S. C. R. 710.	Judgment reversed in part.
Dwyer v. Town of Port Arthur (19 A. R. 555).	22 S. C. R. 241.	Judgment reversed.
Dyment v. Thomson (12 A. R. 659) 9 O. R. 566.	13 S. C. R. 303.	Judgment affirmed.
Electric Despatch Co. of Toronto v. Bell Telephone Co.(17 A. R. 292)17 O. R. 495	20 S. C. R. 83.	Judgment affirmed.
Erb v. Great Western Ry. Co. (2 A. R. 446) 42 Q. B. 90.	5 S. C. R. 179.	Judgment affirmed.
Erwin v. Canada Southern Ry. Co. (11 A. R. 306).	13 S. C. R. 162.	Judgment reversed.
Exchange Bank v. Barnes. Exchange Bank v. Springer (13 A. R. 390) }	14 S. C. R. 716.	Judgment affirmed.
Faulds v. Harper (9 A. R. 537) 2 O. R. 405.	11 S. C. R. 639.	Judgment reversed.
Ferguson v. Ferguson (7 A. R. 452) 39 Q. B. 232.	2 S. C. R. 497.	Judgment reversed.
Fitzgerald v. Grand Trunk Ry. Co. (4 A. R. 601) 28 C. P. 586.	5 S. C. R. 204.	Judgment affirmed.
Forrestal v. McDonald, 29 Gr. 300.	9 S. C. R. 12.	Judgment affirmed.
Frey v. Wellington Mutual Ins. Co. (4 A. R. 293) 43 Q. B. 102.	5 S. C. R. 82.	Judgment reversed.
Gage v. Canada Publishing Co. (11 A. R. 402) 6 O. R. 68.	11 S. C. R. 306.	Judgment affirmed.
Gemmill v. Garland (23 C. L. J. 294) 12 O. R. 139.	14 S. C. R. 321.	Judgment affirmed.
Gibbons v. McDonald (18 A. R. 159) 19 O. R. 290.	20 S. C. R. 587.	Judgment affirmed.
Godson & City of Toronto, in re (16 A. R. 452) 16 O. R. 275.	18 S. C. R. 36.	Judgment affirmed.
Goldsmith v. City of London (23 C. L. J. 294) 11 O. R. 26.	16 S. C. R. 231.	Judgment reversed.
Grand Junction Ry. Co. v. Bickford (23 Gr. 302).	1 S. C. R. 696.	Judgment reversed.
Grand Junction Ry. Co. v. Town of Peterboro' (6 A. R. 339) 45 Q. B. 302.	8 S. C. R. 76.	Judgment affirmed.
Grant v. Peoples' Loan & Deposit Co. (17 A. R. 85).	18 S. C. R. 262.	Judgment affirmed.
Gray v. Richford (1 A. R. 112).	2 S. C. R. 431.	Judgment reversed.
Grip Printing & Publishing Co. v. Butterfield (11 A. R. 145).	11 S. C. R. 291.	Judgment reversed.
Halton, County of, v. Grand Trunk Ry. Co. (19 A. R. 252).	21 S. C. R. 716.	Judgment affirmed.'
Hately v. Merchants' Despatch Transportation Co. (12 A. R. 201) 4 O. R. 723.	14 S. C. R. 572.	Judgment affirmed.
Hayes v. Elmsley (19 A. R. 291) 21 O. R. 662.	Not yet reported.	Judgment reversed.
Henderson v. Killey (17 A. R. 456) 14 O. R. 137.	18 S. C. R. 698 sub nom. Osborne v. Henderson	Judgment reversed.
Heward v. O'Donohoe (18 A. R. 529).	19 S. C. R. 341.	Judgment reversed.
Hislop v. Township of McGillivray (15 A. R. 687) 12 O. R. 749.	17 S. C. R. 479.	Judgment affirmed.
Hobbs v. Guardian Assur. Co. Hobbs v. Northern Assur. Co. (11 A. R. 741) 7 O. R. 634 ; 8 O. R. 343. }	12 S. C. R. 631.	Judgment reversed.
Howard v. Bickford (17 C. L. J. 158).	S. C. Dig. 286.	Judgment affirmed.
Howland v. Dominion Bank (15 P. R. 56).	22 S. C. R. 130.	Judgment affirmed.

CASE.	REPORT ON APPEAL.	RESULT OF APPEAL.
Hunter v. Carrick (10 A. R. 449) 28 Gr. 489.	11 S. C. R. 300.	Judgment affirmed.
Huson v. South Norwich (19 A. R. 343).	21 S. C. R. 669.	Judgment as to publication of by-law affirmed; stands for argument on Constitnti'n'l question.
Jellett v. Anderson (7 A. R. 341) 27 Gr. 411.	9 S. C. R. 1.	Judgment reversed.
Johnson v. Western Ins. Co. (4 A. R. 281).	4 S. C. R. 215.	Judgment affirmed.
Johnston v. Oliver, 3 O. R. 26.	S. C. Dig. 651.	Judgment affirmed.
Jones v. Grand Trunk Ry. Co. (16 A. R. 37).	18 S. C. R. 696.	Judgment affirmed.
Keefer v. McKay (9 A. R. 117) 29 Gr. 162.	13 S. C. R. 515 *sub nom.* Merchants' Bank v. Keefer.	Judgment reversed.
Kelly v. Imperial Loan Co. (11 A. R. 526).	11 S. C. R. 516.	Judgment affirmed.
Kloeffer v. Gardner (14 A. R. 60) 10 O. R. 415.	15 S. C. R. 390.	Judgment affirmed,
Langtry v. Dumoulin (7 O. R. 644) 7 O. R. 499.	13 S. C. R. 258.	Judgment affirmed.
Lawlor v. Lawlor (6 A. R. 312).	10 S. C. R. 194.	Judgment reversed.
Lemay v. McRae (16 A. R. 348) 16 O. R. 307.	18 S. C. R. 280.	Judgment affirmed.
Lett v. St. Lawrence & Ottawa Ry. Co. (11 A. R. 1) 1 O. R. 545.	11 S. C. R. 422.	Judgment affirmed, and leave to appeal to Privy Council refused.
Long v. Hancock (12 A. R. 137) 7 O. R. 154).	12 S. C. R. 532.	Judgment reversed.
Maclennan v. Gray (16 A. R. 224) 16 O. R. 321.	18 S. C. R. 553 *sub nom.* Gray v. Coughlin.	Judgment reversed.
Magee v. Gilmour (17 A. R. 27) 17 O. R. 620.	18 S. C. R. 579.	Judgment affirmed.
Maritime Bank v. Stewart (13 P. R. 491) 13 P. R. 86, 262.	20 S. C. R. 105.	Appeal quashed.
Marsh v. Webb (19 A. R. 564) 21 O. R. 281.	Not yet reported.	Judgment affirmed.
Marshall v. McRae (17 A. R. 139) 16 O. R. 495.	19 S. C. R. 10.	Judgment reversed.
Mead v. O'Keefe (15 A. R. 103).	17 S. C. R. 596 *sub nom.* O'Keefe v. Curran.	Judgment reversed.
Merchants' Bank v. Lucas (15 A. R. 573) 13 O. R. 520.	18 S. C. R. 704.	Judgment affirmed.
Merchants' Bank v. McKay, 12 O. R. 498.	15 S. C. R. 672.	Judgment affirmed.
Merchants' Bank v. Moffatt (5 O. R. 122).	11 S. C. R. 46.	Judgment affirmed.
Miller v. Confederation Life Assoc. (14 A. R. 218) 11 O. R. 120.	14 S. C. R. 330.	Judgment affirmed.
Milloy v. Kerr (3 A. R. 350) 43 Q. B. 78.	8 S. C. R. 474.	Judgment affirmed.
Molson's Bank v. Halter (16 A. R. 323).	18 S. C. R. 88.	Judgment affirmed.
Moore v. Connecticut Mutual Ins. Co. (3 A. R. 230) 41 Q. B. 497.	6 S. C. R. 634, aff. by P. C. 6 App. Cas. 644.	Judgment reversed.
Moore v. Jackson (19 A. R. 483) 20 O. R. 652.	22 S. C. R. 210.	Judgment reversed.
Moxley v. Canada Atlantic Ry. Co. (14 A. R. 309).	15 S. C. R. 145.	Judgment affirmed.

CASE.	REPORT ON APPEAL.	RESULT OF APPEAL.
Murphy v. Kingston & Pembroke Ry. Co. 11 O. R. 320, 582.	17 S. C. R. 582.	Judgment affirmed.
Murray v. Canada Central Ry. Co. (7 A. R. 646).	8 S. C. R. 313.	Judgment affirmed.
MacDonald v. Georgian Bay Lumber Co. (2 A. R. 36) 24 Gr. 356.	2 S. C. R. 364.	Judgment affirmed.
MacDougall, *in re* (15 A. R. 150) 13 O. R. 204.	18 S. C. R. 203 *sub nom.* MacDougall v. Law Soc'y of Upper Can.	Judgment reversed.
McCrae v. Whyte (7 A. R. 103).	9 S. C. R. 22.	Judgment affirmed.
McDonald v. Crombie (10 A. R. 92) 2 O. R. 243.	11 S. C. R. 107.	Judgment affirmed.
McDonald v. McCall (12 A. R. 593) 9 O. R. 185.	13 S. C. R. 247.	Judgment affirmed.
McDonald v. McDonald (17 A. R. 192).	21 S. C. R. 201.	Judgment affirmed.
McDonald v. Worthington (7 A. R. 531).	9 S. C. R. 327.	Judgment affirmed.
McGugan v. McGugan (19 A. R. 56) 21 O. R. 289.	21 S. C. R. 267.	Appeal dismissed; decision of Court of Appeal not to be interfered with even if appealable.
McIntyre v. McCracken (1 A. R. 1) 37 Q. B. 422.	1 S. C. R. 479.	Judgment reversed.
McKenna v. McNamee (14 A. R. 339).	15 S. C. R. 311.	Judgment affirmed.
McKenzie v. Kittridge (27 C. P. 65) 24 C. P. 1, 145.	4 S. C. R. 368.	Judgment affirmed.
McLaren v. Caldwell (6 A. R. 456) 5 A. R. 363.	8 S. C. R. 435; aff. by P. C. 9 App. Cas. 392.	Judgment reversed, but restored on further app.
McLean v. Garland (10 A. R. 405) 32 C. P. 524.	13 S. C. R. 366.	Judgment reversed.
McMillan v. Barton (19 A. R. 602).	20 S. C. R. 404.	Judgment affirmed.
McMillan v. Grand Trunk Ry. Co. (15 A. R. 14) 12 O. R. 103.	16 S. C. R. 543.	Judgment reversed, and leave to appeal to Privy Council refused.
McQueen v. Phœnix Mutual Ins. Co. (4 A. R. 289) 29 C. P. 511.	4 S. C. R. 660.	Judgment reversed.
Nasmith v. Manning (5 A. R. 126) 29 C. P. 34.	5 S. C. R. 417.	Judgment affirmed. Leave to appeal to Privy Council granted but not procedeed with.
Neill v. Travellers' Ins. Co. (7 A. R. 570) 31 C. P. 394.	12 S. C. R. 55.	Judgment affirmed.
Nelles v. White, 29 Gr. 338.	11 S. C. R. 587.	Judgment affirmed.
New Hamburg v. County of Waterloo (20 A. R. 1) 22 O. R. 193.	22 S. C. R. 296.	Judgment reversed.
Nicholls v. Cumming (26 C. P. 323) 25 C. P. 169.	1 S. C. R. 395.	Judgment reversed.
North Ontario Election Case (Hodge. El. Cas. 785).	4 S. C. R. 430.	Judgment reversed.
North York Election Case (32 C. P. 458).	S. C. Dig. 682.	Appeal dismissed by consent.
Norvell v. Canada Southern Ry. Co. (9 A. R. 310).	S. C. Dig. 34.	Judgment reversed.
O'Donohoe, *in re* (14 P. R. 317) 12 P. R. 612.	19 S. C. R. 356 *sub. nom.* O'Donohoe v. Beatty.	Judgment affirmed.
O'Mearn v. City of Ottawa (15 A. R. 75) 11 O. R. 603.	14 S. C. R. 742.	Judgment affirmed.

CASE.	REPORT ON APPEAL.	RESULT OF APPEAL.
Ontario Loan & Debenture Co. v. Hobbs (16 A. R. 255) 15 O. R. 440.	18 S. C. R. 483.	Judgment reversed.
O'Sullivan v. Harty (10 A. R. 76).	11 S. C. R. 322.	Judgment affirmed.
O'Sullivan v. Lake (15 A. R. 711) 15 O. R. 544.	16 S. C. R. 636.	Appeal quashed, being from a judgment given in exercise of discretion.
Pardee v. Lloyd (5 A. R. 1) 26 Gr. 375.	S. C. Dig. 35 *sub nom.* Bickford v. Lloyd.	Judgment affirmed.
Page v. Austin (7 A. R. 1) 30 C. P. 108.	10 S. C. R. 132.	Judgment affirmed.
Parsons v. Citizens' Ins. Co. (4 A. R. 96) 43 Q. B. 261. Parsons v. Queen Ins. Co. (4 A. R. 103) 43 Q. B. 271.	4 S. C. R. 215.	Judgment affirmed, but reversed on further appeal, 7 App. Cas. 96, as to validity of Ontario Insurance Act.
Parsons v. Standard Ins. Co. (4 A. R. 326) 43 Q. B. 603.	5 S. C. R. 233.	Judgment reversed.
Partlo v. Todd (14 A. R. 444) 12 O. R. 171.	17 S. C. R. 196.	Judgment affirmed.
Peck v. Powell. Powell v. Peck (8 A. R.498) 26 Gr. 322.	11 S. C. R. 494.	Judgment reversed in Peck v. Powell. Affirmed in Powell v. Peck.
Peek v. Shields (6 A. R. 639) 31 C. P. 112	8 S. C. R. 579.	Judgment affirmed by equal division.
Peterkin v. McFarlane (9 A. R. 429).	13 S. C. R. 677 *sub nom.* Rose v. Peterkin.	Judgment affirmed.
Petrie v. Guelph Lumber Co. (11 A. R. 336) 2 O. R. 218.	11 S. C. R. 450.	Judgment affirmed.
Plumb v. Steinhoff (11 A. R. 788) 2 O. R. 614	14 S. C. R. 739.	Judgment affirmed.
Purcell v. Bergin (20 A. R. 535).	———	Stands for judgment.
Purdom v. Nichol (15 A. R. 244).	15 S. C. R. 610 *sub nom* Purdom v. Baechler.	Judgment reversed.
Reg. v. Amer (42 Q. B. 391).	2 S. C. R. 592.	Appeal quashed.
Reg. v. County of Wellington (17 A. R. 421) 17 O. R. 615.	19 S. C. R. 510 *sub. nom.* Quirt v. The Queen.	Judgment affirmed.
Reg. v. Howland (14 A. R. 184) 11 O. R. 633.	16 S. C. R. 197 *sub nom. in re* O'Brien.	Judgment reversed.
Reg. v. St. Catharines' Milling Co. (13 A. R. 148) 10 O. R. 196.	13 S. C. R. 577 ; aff. by P. C. 14 App. Cas. 46	Judgment affirmed.
Reg. v. Taylor (36 Q. B. 183, 218).	1 S. C. R. 65.	Appeal quashed.
Robinson v. Harris (19 A. R. 134) 21 O. R. 43.	21 S. C. R. 390.	Judgment reversed.
Rose v. Hickey (3 A. R. 309).	S. C. Dig. 534.	Judgment affirmed.
Rosenberger v. Grand Trunk Ry. Co. (8 A. R. 482) 32 C. P. 349.	9 S. C. R. 311.	Judgment affirmed.
Ryan v. Clarkson (16 A. R. 311).	17 S. C. R. 251.	Judgment affirmed.
Ryan v. Ryan (4 A. R. 563) 29 C. P. 449.	5 S. C. R. 387.	Judgment reversed.
Samo v. Gore District Mutual Ins. Co. (1 A. R. 545) 26 C. P. 405.	2 S. C. R. 411.	Judgment reversed.
Sanderson v. McKercher (13 A. R. 561).	15 S. C. R. 296.	Judgment reversed.
Schroeder v. Rooney (11 A. R. 673).	S. C. Dig. 403.	Judgment affirmed.
Scott v. Benedict (22 C. L. J. 43) 5 O. R. 1.	14 S. C. R. 735.	Judgment affirmed.

CASE.	REPORT ON APPEAL.	RESULT OF APPEAL.
Scribner v. Kinloch (12 A. R. 367) 2 O. R. 265.	14 S. C. R. 77.	Judgment affirmed.
Seymour v. Lynch (14 A. R. 738) 7 O. R. 471.	15 S. C. R. 341.	Judgment affirmed by equal division.
Shairp v. Lakefield Lumber Co. (17 A. R. 322).	19 S. C. R. 657.	Judgment affirmed.
Shannon v. Hastings Mutual Ins. Co. (2 A. R. 81) 26 C. P. 380.	2 S. C. R. 394.	Judgment affirmed.
Sibbald v. Grand Trunk Ry. Co. Tremayne v. Grand Trunk Ry. Co. (18 A. R. 184) 19 O. R. 164.	20 S. C. R. 259.	Judgment affirmed.
Smart, *in re* (12 P. R. 635) 12 P. R. 312, 435.	16 S. C. R. 396.	Appeal quashed for not being brought in time.
Smith v. Goldie (7 A. R. 628.	9 S. C. R. 46.	Judgment reversed.
Smith v. London Ins. Co. (14 A. R. 328) 11 O. R. 38.	15 S. C. R. 69.	Judgment affirmed.
Smith v. Merchants' Bank (8 A. R. 15) 28 Gr. 629.	8 S. C. R. 512.	Judgment reversed.
Sombra, Township of, v. Township of Chatham (18 A. R. 252).	21 S. C. R. 305.	Judgment reversed.
South Ontario Election Case (Hodg. El. Cas. 751).	3 S. C. R. 641.	Judgment affirmed.
Stammers v. O'Donohoe (8 A. R. 101) 28 Gr. 207.	11 S. C. R. 358.	Judgment affirmed.
Standard Fire Ins. Co. *in re* Customs Case (12 A. R. 486) 7 O. R. 201, 448.	12 S. C. R. 644.	Judgment affirmed.
Standly v. Perry (2 A. R. 195) 23 Gr. 507.	3 S. C. R. 356.	Judgment affirmed.
Stephens v. Gordon (19 A. R. 176).	22 S. C. R. 61.	Judgment affirmed.
Stevenson v. Davis (19 A. R. 591) 21 O. R. 642.	Not yet reported.	Judgment reversed.
Stewart v. Lees, 24 Gr. 433.	S. C. Dig. 93.	Judgment affirmed.
St. John v. Rykert (4 A. R. 213) 26 Gr. 249.	10 S. C. R. 278.	Judgment affirmed.
Sutherland v. Cox (15 A. R. 541) 6 O. R. 505.	S. C. Dig. 9.	Judgment affirmed.
Taylor v. Taylor (1 A. R. 245) 23 Gr. 496.	2 S. C. R. 616 *sub. nom.* Taylor v. Wallbridge.	Judgment reversed.
Thorold v. Neelon (18 A. R. 658) 20 O. R. 86.	Not yet reported.	Judgment reversed.
Trust & Loan Co. v. Lawrason (6 A. R. 286) 45 Q. B. 176.	10 S. C. R. 679.	Judgment affirmed.
Trust & Loan Co. v. Ruttan (1 A. R. 26). 32 Q. B. 222.	1 S. C. R. 564.	Judgment reversed.
Union Fire Ins. Co. *in re* (13 A. R. 268) 10 O. R. 489.	14 S. C. R. 624.	Judgment reversed.
Victoria, County of, v. County of Peterboro' (15 A. R. 617) 15 O. R. 446.	S. C. Dig. 558.	Judgment affirmed.
Virgo and City of Toronto, *in re* (20 A. R. 435).	——	Stands for judgment.
Vogel v. Grand Trunk Ry. Co. Morton v. G. T. Ry. Co. (10 A. R. 162) 2 O. R. 197.	11 S. C. R. 612.	Judgment affirmed.
Wallbridge v. Gaujot (14 A. R. 460).	15 S. C. R. 650 *sub nom.* Palmer v. Wallbridge	Judgment affirmed.
Walmsley v. Griffith (10 A. R. 327).	13 S. C. R. 434.	Judgment affirmed.
Warin v. London & Canadian Loan Co. (12 A. R. 327) 7 O. R. 706.	14 S. C. R. 232.	Judgment affirmed.
Warnock v. Kloepfer (15 A. R. 324) 14 O. R. 288	18 S. C. R. 701.	Judgment affirmed.

CASE.	REPORT ON APPEAL.	RESULT OF APPEAL.
Waterous Engine Works Co. v. Town of Palmerston (19 A. R. 47) 20 O. R. 411.	21 S. C. R. 556.	Judgment affirmed.
Watt v. City of London (19 A. R. 675).	22 S. C. R. 300.	Judgment affirmed.
West v. Corporation of Parkdale. Carroll v. Corporation of Parkdale (12 A. R. 393) 7 O. R. 270 ; 8 O. R. 59.	12 S. C. R. 250 ; affirmed by P. C. 12 App. Cas. 602.	Judgment reversed.
West Huron Election Case (1 O. R. 433).	8 S. C. R. 126.	Judgment reversed.
West Northumberland Election Case (1 Ont. El. Case 32).	10 S. C. R. 635.	Judgment reversed.
Western Assur. Co. v. Ontario Coal Co. (19 A. R. 41) 20 O. R. 295 ; 19 O. R. 462.	21 S. C. R. 383.	Judgment affirmed.
Whiting v. Hovey (13 A. R. 7) 9 O. R. 314.	14 S. C. R. 515.	Judgment affirmed.
Wiley v. Smith (1 A. R. 179.)	2 S. C. R. 1.	Judgment affirmed.
Wilkins v. McLean (13 A. R. 467) 10 O. R. 58.	14 S. C. R. 22.	Judgment reversed.
Williams v. Corby (3 A. R. 626.	7 S. C. R. 470.	Judgment reversed.
Wright v. Bell (18 A. R. 25).	S. C. Dig. 880 sub nom. Houghton v. Bell	Judgment reversed.
Wright v. London Life Assur. Co. (5 A. R. 218) 29 C. P. 221.	5 S. C. R. 466.	Judgment affirmed.
Wright v. Synod of Huron (9 A. R. 411) 29 Gr. 348.	11 S. C. R. 95.	Judgment affirmed.
Wyld v. Liverpool, London & Globe Ins. Co. (23 Gr. 442) 21 Gr. 458.	1 S. C. R. 604.	Judgment affirmed by equal division.
York, County of, v. Toronto Gravel Co. (11 A. R. 765) 3 O. R. 584.	12 S. C. R. 517.	Judgment affirmed.
Young v. Midland Railway (19 A. R. 265) 16 O. R. 738.	22 S. C. R. 190.	Judgment affirmed.

CASES IN THE COURT OF CHANCERY FOR ONTARIO CARRIED TO THE COURT OF APPEAL.

CASE.	REPORT ON APPEAL.	RESULT OF APPEAL.
Abell v. McPherson (17 Gr. 23).	18 Gr. 437.	Judgment affirmed.
Adamson v. Adamson (28 Gr. 226).	7 A. R. 592. aff. by Sup. Ct. 12 S. C. R. 563.	Judgment affirmed.
Allan v. McTavish (28 Gr. 539).	8 A. R. 440.	Judgment reversed.
Anderson v. Bell (29 Gr. 452).	8 A. R. 531.	Judgment affirmed.
Arkell v. Wilson (5 Gr. 470).	7 Gr. 270.	Judgment affirmed.
Arnold v. McLean (4 Gr. 337).	6 Gr. 242.	Judgment reversed.
Arran v. Annabel (15 Gr. 701).	17 Gr. 163.	Judgment reversed on re-hearing.
Atty.-Gen, v. Grasset (5 Gr. 412) (6 Gr. 485).	6 Gr. 200 ; 8 Gr. 130.	Judgment affirmed in both cases.
Atty.-Gen. v. Walker (25 Gr. 233).	3 A. R. 195.	Judgment affirmed.
Atty.-Gen. of Ontario v. International Bridge Co. (28 Gr. 65).	6 A. R. 537.	Judgment reversed.
Atty.-Gen. of Ontario v. O'Reilly (26 Gr. 126).	6 A. R. 576 ; reversed by Sup. Ct. sub nom. Mercer v. Atty.-Gen. 5 S.C.R. 538; restored by P. C. 8 App. Cas. 767.	Judgment affirmed.
Bank of Montreal v. Hopkins (9 Gr. 495).	2 E. & A. 458.	Judgment reversed.
Bank of Montreal v. Thomson (9 Gr. 51).	2 E. & A. 239.	Judgment affirmed.
Bank of Toronto v. Fanning (17 Gr. 514).	18 Gr. 391.	Judgment affirmed.
Bank of Upper Canada v. Beatty (9 Gr. 321).	2 E. & A. 502.	Judgment reversed.
Bank of Upper Canada v. Thomas (9 Gr. 321).	2 E. & A. 502.	Judgment affirmed.
Barker v. Eccles (17 Gr. 631).	18 Gr. 440, 523.	Judgment affirmed.
Barnhart v. Patterson (1 Gr. 459).	3 Gr. 1, sub nom. Green-shields v. Patterson ; affirmed by P. C.	Judgment affirmed.
Beckitt v. Wragg (6 Gr. 454).	7 Gr. 290.	Judgment reversed.
Bell v. Lee (28 Gr. 150).	8 A. R. 185.	Judgment reversed in part.
Billington v. Provincial Ins. Co. (24 Gr. 250).	2 A. R. 159, aff. by Sup. Ct. 3 S. C. R. 182.	Judgment reversed.
Black v. Black (9 Gr. 403)	2 E. & A. 419.	Judgment reversed.

CASE	REPORT ON APPEAL	RESULT OF APPEAL
Blake v. Kirkpatrick (27 Gr. 86).	6 A. R. 212.	Judgment reversed.
Boulton v. Church Soc. Diocese of Toronto (14 Gr. 123).	15 Gr. 450.	Judgment affirmed.
Bown v. West (1 O. S. 287).	1 E. & A. 117.	Judgment affirmed.
Box v. Provincial Ins. Co. (15 Gr. 337,552).	18 Gr. 280.	Judgment reversed.
Brown v. Kingsmill (1 O. S. 172).	1 E. & A. 148 *sub nom.* Brown v. Smart.	Judgment reversed.
Buchanan v. Smith (17 Gr. 208).	18 Gr. 41.	Judgment affirmed on re-hearing.
Buchanan v. Tiffany (1 Gr. 98).	1 Gr. 257.	Judgment affirmed.
Butler v. Church (16 Gr. 205).	18 Gr. 190.	Judgment affirmed.
Butler v. Standard Ins. Co. (26 Gr. 341).	4 A. R. 391.	Judgment affirmed.
Caldwell v. Hall (6 U. C. L. J. 141).	8 U. C. L. J. 93.	Judgment affirmed.
Cameron v. Campbell (27 Gr. 307).	18 C. L. J. 273.	Judgment affirmed.
Cameron v. Kerr (7 P. R. 265).	3 A. R. 30.	Judgment affirmed.
Campbell v. McDougall (26 Gr. 380).	5 A. R. 503; aff. by Sup. Ct. 6 S. C. R. 502.	Judgment reversed.
Canada Fire & Marine Ins. Co. v. Western Assur. Co. (26 Gr. 264).	5 A. R. 244.	Judgment affirmed.
Cannon v. Toronto Com. Exchange (27 Gr. 23).	5 A. R. 263.	Judgment affirmed.
Chandler v. Ford (6 Gr. 607).	8 Gr. 85.	Judgment reversed.
Chisholm, *in re* (17 Gr. 403).	18 Gr. 467.	Judgment affirmed.
Chisholm v. Sheldon (2 Gr. 178) 1 Gr. 108.	3 Gr. 655.	Judgment reversed.
Commercial Bank v. Bank of Upper Canada (7 Gr. 250).	7 Gr. 423.	Judgment affirmed.
Cotton v. Corby (7 Gr. 50).	8 Gr. 98.	Judgment affirmed.
Craig v. Craig (24 Gr. 573).	2 A. R. 583.	Judgment reversed.
Crippen v. Ogilvie (15 Gr. 490).	18 Gr. 253.	Judgment affirmed.
Crooks v. Torrance (6 Gr. 518).	8 Gr. 220.	Judgment affirmed.
Curry v. Curry (26 Gr. 1).	4 A. R. 63; aff. by Sup. Ct. S. C. Dig. 778.	Judgment affirmed.
Davidson v. Boomer (17 Gr. 509).	18 Gr. 475.	Judgment affirmed.
Davidson v. McGuire (27 Gr. 483).	7 A. R. 98.	Judgment affirmed.
Denison v. Denison (17 Gr. 219).	18 Gr. 41, re-hearing.	Judgment affirmed.
Dilke v. Douglas (26 Gr. 99).	5 A. R. 63.	Judgment reversed.
Direct Cable Co. v. Dominion Telegraph Co. (28 Gr. 648).	8 A. R. 416.	Judgment affirmed.
Dominion Loan Soc. v. Darling (27 Gr. 68).	5 A. R. 576.	Judgment affirmed.
Duff v. Canada Mutual Fire Ins. Co. (27 Gr. 391).	6 A. R. 238.	Judgment affirmed.

CASE.	REPORT ON APPEAL.	RESULT OF APPEAL.
Dumble v. Dumble (29 Gr. 274).	8 A. R. 476.	Judgment reversed.
Dundas, Town of, v. Hamilton & Milton Road Co. (17 Gr. 31).	18 Gr. 311.	Judgment reversed.
Earle v. McAlpine (27 Gr. 161).	6 A. R. 145.	Judgment affirmed.
Emmett v. Quinn (27 Gr. 420).	7 A. R. 306.	Judgment reversed.
Ewart v. Steven (16 Gr. 193).	18 Gr. 35.	Judgment reversed.
Georgian Bay Trans. Co. v. Fisher (27 Gr. 346).	5 A. R. 383.	Judgment reversed.
Gilleland v. Wadsworth (23 Gr. 547).	1 A. R. 82.	Judgment reversed.
Glass v. Hope (14 Gr. 484).	16 Gr. 420.	Judgment affirmed.
Goyeau v. Great Western Ry. Co. (25 Gr. 62).	3 A. R. 412.	Judgment reversed.
Grand Junction Ry. Co. v. Bickford (12 L. J. N. S. 180).	23 Gr. 302.	Judgment affirmed.
Grant v. Brown (12 Gr. 52).	13 Gr. 256.	Judgment reversed.
Gray v. Springer (5 Gr. 242).	7 Gr. 276.	Judgment reversed.
Graves v. Smith (6 Gr. 306).	2 E. & A. 9 *sub nom.* Henderson v. Graves.	Judgment affirmed.
Great Western Ry. Co. v. Desjardines Canal Co. (9 Gr. 503).	2 E. & A. 330.	Judgment reversed.
Green v. Provincial Ins. Co. (26 Gr. 354).	4 A. R. 521.	Judgment affirmed.
Greet v. Citizens' Ins. Co. Greet v. Royal Ins. Co. (27 Gr. 121). }	5 A. R. 596.	Judgment reversed.
Greet v. Mercantile Ins. Co. (27 Gr. 121).	5 A. R. 596.	Judgment affirmed.
Griffith v. Brown (26 Gr. 503).	5 A. R. 303.	Judgment reversed.
Hart v. McQuesten (21 Gr. 242).	22 Gr. 133.	Judgment reversed.
Heenan v. Dewar (17 Gr. 638).	18 Gr. 438.	Judgment affirmed.
Henrihan v. Gallagher (9 Gr. 488).	2 E. & A. 338.	Judgment affirmed.
Hill v. Rutherford (9 Gr. 207).	9 U. C. L. J. 172.	Judgment affirmed.
Holmes v. Matthews (3 Gr. 379).	5 Gr. 1. aff. by Pr. Coun. 9 Moo. P. C. 413.	Judgment reversed.
Hunter v. Carrick (28 Gr. 489).	10 A. R. 449. aff. by Sup. Ct. 11 S. C. R. 300.	Judgment reversed.
International Bridge Co. v. Canada Southern Ry. Co. (28 Gr. 114).	7 A. R. 226.	Judgment affirmed.
Jellett v. Anderson (27 Gr. 411).	7 A. R. 341; rev. by Sup. Ct. 9 S. C. R. 1.	Judgment affirmed, but reversed on further appeal.
Jessup v. Grand Trunk Ry. Co. (28 Gr. 583).	7 A. R. 128.	Judgment reversed.
Joseph v. Heaton (5 Gr. 636).	1 E. & A. 292 *sub nom.* Topping v. Joseph.	Judgment reversed.
Kay v. Wilson (24 Gr. 212).	2 A. R. 133.	Judgment affirmed.

CASE.	REPORT ON APPEAL.	RESULT OF APPEAL.
Keefer v. McKay (29 Gr. 162).	9 A. R. 117 ; rev. by Sup. Ct. 13 S. C. R. 515, sub nom. Merchants' Bank v. Keefer.	Judgment affirmed by equal division, and reversed on further appeal.
Kiely v. Kiely (25 Gr. 463).	3 A. R. 438-	Judgment reversed.
Kilbourn v. Arnold (27 Gr. 429).	6 A. R. 158.	Judgment reversed.
Kirkpatrick v. Lyster (13 Gr. 323).	16 Gr. 17.	Judgment affirmed.
Lavin v. Lavin (27 Gr. 567).	7 A. R. 197.	Judgment affirmed.
Lindsay Petroleum Co. v. Hurd (16 Gr. 147).	17 Gr. 115 ; rev. by Pr. Conn. L. R. 5 P. C. 221.	Judgment reversed in part, but restored on further appeal.
Livingstone v. Western Assur. Co. (14 Gr. 461).	16 Gr. 9.	Judgment reversed.
Livingston v. Wood (27 Gr. 515).	17 C. L. J. 168.	Judgment affirmed.
Lowson v. Canada Farmers' Ins. Co. (28 Gr. 525).	6 A. R. 512.	Judgment reversed.
Macdonell v. McKay (15 Gr. 391).	18 Gr. 98.	Judgment reversed.
Martin v. Martin (12 Gr. 500).	15 Gr. 586.	Judgment affirmed.
Mason & Scott in re (21 Gr. 629).	22 Gr. 592.	Judgment reversed.
Moffatt v. Board of Education of Carleton Place (26 Gr. 590).	5 A. R. 197.	Judgment affirmed.
Mossop v. Mason (17 Gr. 360).	18 Gr. 453.	Judgment affirmed.
Mulholland v. Williamson (12 Gr. 91).	14 Gr. 291.	Judgment reversed.
Munro v. Smart (26 Gr. 310).	4 A. R. 449.	Judgment reversed.
Murray, in re. Purdom v. Murray (29 Gr. 443).	9 A. R. 369.	Judgment reversed.
McDonald v. Forrestal (29 Gr. 300).	None ; aff. by Sup. Ct. 9 S. C. R. 12.	Judgment affirmed.
McDonald v. Georgian Bay Lumber Co. (24 Gr. 356).	2 A. R. 36 ; aff. by Sup. Ct. 2 S. C. R. 364.	Judgment reversed.
McDonald v. McDonald (14 Gr. 545).	16 Gr. 37.	Judgment reversed.
McGregor v. Rapelje (17 Gr. 38).	18 Gr. 446.	Judgment affirmed.
McKenzie v. Yielding (11 Gr. 406).	13 Gr. 259.	Judgment affirmed.
McPherson v. McKay (26 Gr. 141).	4 A. R. 501.	Judgment affirmed.
Nelles v. Bank of Montreal (28 Gr. 449). White v. Nelles (29 Gr. 338).	7 A. R. 743. None ; judg't on appeal aff. by Sup. Ct. 11 S. C. R. 587.	Judgment affirmed. Judgment affirmed.
Newton v. Ontario Bank (13 Gr. 652).	15 Gr. 283.	Judgment affirmed.
Norris v. Meadows (28 Gr. 334).	7 A. R. 237.	Judgment affirmed.
Pardee v. Lloyd (26 Gr. 374).	5 A. R. 1 ; aff. by Sup. Ct. sub nom. Bickford v. Lloyd, S. C. Dig. 35	Judgment reversed.
Parke v. Riley (12 Gr. 69).	3 E. & A. 215.	Judgment affirmed.

M.D.—2

CASE.	REPORT ON APPEAL.	RESULT OF APPEAL.
Parkhurst v. Roy (27 Gr. 361).	7 A. R. 614.	Judgment affirmed.
Paul v. Blackwood (3 Gr. 394).	4 Gr. 550.	Judgment reversed.
Peck v. Powell } (26 Gr. 322). Powell v. Peck }	8 A. R. 498; rev. by Sup. Ct. in Peck v. Powell, 11 S. C. R. 494.	Judgment reversed, but restored in Peck v. Powell on further appeal.
Pierce v. Canavan (28 Gr. 356).	7 A. R. 187.	Judgment affirmed.
Rastall v. Atty.-Gen. (17 Gr. 1)·	18 Gr. 138.	Judgment reversed.
Read v. Smith (14 Gr. 250).	16 Gr. 52.	Judgment affirmed.
Reid v. Whitehead (10 Gr. 446).	2 E. & A. 580.	Judgment reversed.
Rieker v. Ricker (27 Gr. 576).	7 A. R. 282.	Judgment reversed.
Sanderson v. Burdett (16 Gr. 119).	18 Gr. 417.	Judgment affirmed.
Saylor v. Cooper (18 C. L. J. 262).	19 C. L. J. 348.	Judgment affirmed.
Silverthorn v. Hunter (26 Gr. 390).	5 A. R. 157.	Judgment affirmed.
Sinclair v. Dewar (17 Gr. 621).	19 Gr. 59.	Judgment reversed,
Smiles v. Belford (23 Gr. 590).	1 A. R. 436.	Judgment affirmed.
Smith v. Merchants' Bank (28 Gr. 629).	8 A. R. 15.	Judgment reversed.
Smith v. Ratte (13 Gr. 696).	15 Gr. 473.	Judgment affirmed.
Stammers v. O'Donohoe (28 Gr. 207).	8 A. R. 161; aff. by Sup. Ct. 11 S. C. R. 358.	Judgment affirmed.
Standly v. Perry (23 Gr. 507).	2 A. R. 195; aff. by Sup. Ct. 3 S. C. R. 356.	Judgment reversed.
Staunton v. Western Assur. Co. (21 Gr. 578).	23 Gr. 81.	Judgment affirmed.
Stephens v. Simpson (12 Gr. 493).	15 Gr. 594.	Judgment affirmed.
St. John v. Rykert (26 Gr. 249).	4 A. R. 213; aff. by Sup. Ct. 10 S. C. R. 278.	Judgment reversed.
Taylor v. Taylor (23 Gr. 496).	1 A. R. 245, rev. by Sup. Ct. 2 S. C. R. 616 *sub nom.* Taylor v. Wallbridge.	Judgment affirmed, but reversed on further appeal.
Thomson v. Torrance (28 Gr. 253).	9 A. R. 1.	Judgment affirmed.
Totten v. Douglas (16 Gr. 243).	18 Gr. 341.	Judgment reversed.
Victoria Mutual Ins. Co. v. Bethune (23 Gr. 568).	1 A. R. 398.	Judgment affirmed.
Walker v. Provincial Ins. Co. (7 Gr. 137).	8 Gr. 217.	Judgment affirmed.
Walker v. Walton (24 Gr. 209).	1 A. R. 579.	Judgment reversed.
Wallace, Township of, v. Great Western Ry. Co. (25 Gr. 86).	3 A. R. 44.	Judgment affirmed.
Washburn v. Ferris (14 Gr. 516).	16 Gr. 76.	Judgment affirmed.
Watson v. Lindsay (27 Gr. 253).	6 A. R. 609.	Judgment affirmed.

CASE.	REPORT ON APPEAL.	RESULT OF APPEAL.
Watson v. Mason (22 Gr. 180).	22 Gr. 574.	Judgment reversed.
Watson v. Munro (6 Gr. 385) 5 Gr. 662.	8 Gr. 60.	Judgment reversed.
Weir v. Mathieson (11 Gr. 383).	3 E. & A. 123.	Judgment reversed.
Western Assur. Co. v. Provincial Ins. Co. (26 Gr. 561).	5 A. R. 190.	Judgment affirmed.
Whitby, Town of, v. Liscombe (22 Gr. 203).	23 Gr. 1.	Judgment affirmed.
Whitehead v. Buffalo & Lake Huron Ry. Co. (7 Gr. 351).	8 Gr. 157.	Judgment varied.
Wilson v. Beatty. *In re* Donovan (29 Gr. 280).	9 A. R. 149.	Judgment reversed.
Workman v. Robb (28 Gr. 243).	7 A. R. 389.	Judgment affirmed.
Worswick v. Canada Fire & Marine Ins. Co. (25 Gr. 282).	3 A. R. 487.	Judgment affirmed.
Wright v. Morgan (24 Gr. 457).	1 A. R. 613.	Judgment reversed.
Wright v. Synod of Huron (29 Gr. 348).	9 A. R. 411 ; aff. by Sup. Ct. 11 S. C. R. 95.	Judgment reversed.
Wyld v. Liverpool, London & Globe Ins. Co. (21 Gr. 458).	23 Gr. 442 ; aff. by Sup. Ct. 1 S. C. R. 604.	Judgment affirmed.
Yates v. Great Western Ry. Co. (24 Gr. 495).	2 A. R. 226.	Judgment reversed.

CASES IN THE COURT OF QUEEN'S BENCH FOR ONTARIO CARRIED TO THE COURT OF APPEAL.

CASE.	REPORT ON APPEAL.	RESULT OF APPEAL.
Agricultural Investment Co. v. Federal Bank (45 Q. B. 214).	6 A. R. 192.	Judgment affirmed.
Alexander v. Toronto & Nipissing Ry. Co. (33 Q. B. 474).	35 Q. B. 453.	Judgment affirmed.
Allan v. McTavish (41 Q. B. 567).	2 A. R. 278.	Judgment reversed.
Backus v. Smith (44 Q. B. 428).	5 A. R. 341.	Judgment reversed.
Ball v. Parker (39 Q. B. 488).	1 A. R. 593.	Judgment affirmed.
Ballagh v. Royal Mutual Fire Ins. Co. (44 Q. B. 70).	5 A. R. 87.	Judgment reversed.
Bank of Toronto v. Nixon (43 Q. B. 447).	4 A. R. 346.	Judgment reversed.
Barber v. Morton (45 Q. B. 386).	7 A. R. 114.	Judgment reversed.
Barker v. Torrance (30 Q. B. 43).	31 Q. B. 561.	Judgment affirmed.
Barned's Banking Co. v. Reynolds (40 Q. B. 435).	3 A. R. 371; rev. by Sup. Ct. S. C. Dig. 170.	Judgment reversed, but restored on further appeal.
Bell v. McKindsey (23 Q. B. 162).	3 E. & A. 1.	Judgment affirmed.
Boulton v. Smith (17 Q. B. 400).	18 Q. B. 458.	Judgment affirmed.
Brooks & County of Haldimand, in re (41 Q. B. 381).	3 A. R. 73.	Judgment reversed.
Brown v. Great Western Ry. Co. (40 Q. B. 333).	2 A. R. 64; aff. by Sup. Ct. 3 S. C. R. 159.	Judgment affirmed.
Burgess v. Bank of Montreal (42 Q. B. 212).	3 A. R. 66.	Judgment affirmed.
Burritt v. Hamilton (17 Q. B. 443).	18 Q. B. 461.	Judgment reversed.
Cameron v. Todd (22 Q. B. 390).	2 E. & A. 434.	Judgment affirmed.
Clark v. Rowe (29 Q. B. 168).	29 Q. B. 302.	Judgment reversed.
Cliswold v. Machell (25 Q. B. 80).	26 Q. B. 422.	Judgment affirmed.
Commercial Bank v. Great Western Ry. Co. (22 Q. B. 233).	2 E. & A. 285; aff. by Pr. Coun. 3 Moo. N. S. 295.	Judgment affirmed.
Cosgrave v. Boyle (45 Q. B. 32).	5 A. R. 458; rev. by Sup. Ct. 6 S. C. R. 165.	Judgment affirmed, but reversed on further appeal.
Cowling v. Dixon (45 Q. B. 94).	5 A. R. 549.	Judgment reversed.
Crathern v. Bell (46 Q. B. 365).	8 A. R. 537.	Judgment affirmed.
Cross v. Currie (43 Q. B. 599).	5 A. R. 31.	Judgment affirmed.

CASE.	REPORT ON APPEAL.	RESULT OF APPEAL.
Darling v. Hitchcock (25 Q. B. 463).	28 Q. B. 439.	Judgment reversed.
Davies v. Home Ins. Co. (24 Q. B. 364).	3 E. & A. 269.	Judgment reversed.
Denison v. Leslie (43 Q. B. 22).	3 A. R. 536.	Judgment affirmed.
Denny v. Montreal Telegraph Co. (42 Q. B. 577).	3 A. R. 628.	Judgment varied.
Doe d. Henderson v. Westover (9 Q. B. 47).	1 E. & A. 465.	Judgment affirmed.
Erb v. Great Western Ry. Co. (42 Q. B. 90).	3 A. R. 446; aff. by Sup. Ct. 5 S. C. R. 179.	Judgment affirmed.
Ferguson v. Ferguson (39 Q. B. 232).	1 A. R. 452; rev. by Sup. Ct. 2 S. C. R. 497.	Judgment reversed, but restored on further appeal.
Frey v. Wellington Mutual Ins. Co. (43 Q. B. 102).	4 A. R. 293, rev. by Sup. Ct. 5 S. C. R. 82.	Judgment affirmed, but reversed on further appeal.
Fryer v. Shield (45 Q. B. 188).	6 A. R. 57.	Judgment reversed.
Gamble v. Great Western Ry. Co. (24 Q. B. 407).	3 E. & A. 163	Judgment affirmed.
Ganton v. Size (22 Q. B. 473).	2 E. & A. 368.	Judgment affirmed.
Gauthier v. Waterloo Ins. Co. (44 Q. B. 490).	6 A. R. 231.	Judgment affirmed.
Gillson v. North Grey Ry. Co. (33 Q. B. 128).	38 Q. B. 475.	Judgment affirmed.
Gossage v. Canada Land & Emigration Co. (24 Q. B. 452).	2 L. J. (N. S.) 90.	Judgment affirmed.
Grand Junction Ry. Co. v. County of Peterboro' (45 Q. B. 302).	6 A. R. 339; aff. by Sup. Ct. 8 S. C. R. 76.	Judgment reversed.
Hall v. Hill (22 Q. B. 578).	2 E. & A. 569.	Judgment affirmed.
Hammond v. McLay (26 Q. B. 434).	28 Q. B. 463.	Judgment reversed.
Harrison v. Pinkney (44 Q. B. 509).	6 A. R. 225.	Judgment affirmed.
Henderson v. Fortune (18 Q. B. 520).	6 U. C. L. J. 197.	Judgment reversed.
Hendrickson v. Queen Ins. Co. (30 Q. B. 108).	31 Q. B. 547.	Judgment affirmed.
High School Board, *in re* (45 Q. B. 160).	8 A. R. 169.	Judgment reversed.
Hood v. Toronto Harbour Commissioners (34 Q. B. 87).	37 Q. B. 72.	Judgment affirmed.
Horseman v. Grand Trunk Ry. Co. (30 Q. B. 130).	31 Q. B. 535.	Judgment affirmed.
Hurd v. Lewis (19 Q. B. 41).	6 U. C. L. J. 197.	Judgment affirmed.
Ingram v. Taylor (46 Q. B. 52).	7 A. R. 216.	Judgment affirmed.
Jones v. Cowden (34 Q. B. 345).	36 Q. B. 395.	Judgment affirmed.
Kings, Municipality of, v. Hughes (17 Q. B. 253).	7 U. C. L. J. 43.	Judgment affirmed.

CASE.	REPORT ON APPEAL.	RESULT OF APPEAL.
Leprohon v. City of Ottawa (40 Q. B. 478).	2 A. R. 522.	Judgment reversed.
Lucas v. Township of Moore (43 Q. B. 334).	3 A. R. 602.	Judgment reversed.
Macdonnell v. MacDonald (19 Q. B. 130).	2 E. & A. 341.	Judgment reversed.
Madden v. Cox (44 Q. B. 542).	5 A. R. 473.	Judgment affirmed by equal division.
Mann v. Western Assur. Co. (19 Q. B. 314).	19 Q. B. 329.	Judgment affirmed.
Marrin v. Stadacona Ins. Co. (43 Q. B. 556).	4 A. R. 330.	Judgment affirmed.
Martin v. Crow (22 Q. B. 485).	2 E. & A. 425.	Judgment reversed.
Mechanics' Building & Saving Soc. v. Gore District Mutual Ins. Co. (40 Q. B. 220).	3 A. R. 151.	Judgment reversed.
Milloy v. Kerr (43 Q. B. 78).	3 A. R. 350 ; aff. by Sup. Ct. 8 S. C. R. 474.	Judgment affirmed.
Mink v. Jarvis (8 Q. B. 397).	13 Q. B. 84.	Judgment affirmed by equal division.
Mitchell v. Goodall (44 Q. B. 398).	5 A. R. 164.	Judgment affirmed.
Moffatt v. Robertson (19 Q. B. 401).	1 E. & A. 459.	Judgment reversed.
Molson's Bank v. McDonald (40 Q. B. 529).	2 A. R. 102.	Judgment affirmed.
Moore v. Connecticut Mutual Ins. Co. (41 Q. B. 497).	3 A. R. 230 ; rev. by Sup. Ct. 6 S. C. R. 634; and by Pr. Coun. 6 App. Cas. 644.	Judgment affirmed, but reversed on further appeal.
McArthur v. Egleson (43 Q. B. 406).	3 A. R. 577.	Judgment affirmed.
McCallum v. Grand Trunk Ry. Co. (30 Q. B. 122).	31 Q. B. 527.	Judgment affirmed.
McCollum v. Wilson (17 Q. B. 572).	18 Q. B. 445.	Judgment reversed.
McEwan v. McLeod (46 Q. B. 235).	9 A. R. 239.	Judgment affirmed.
McHardy v. Township of Ellice (37 Q. B. 580).	1 A. R. 628.	Judgment reversed.
McIntyre v. McCracken (37 Q. B. 422).	1 A. R. 1 ; rev. by Sup. Ct. 1 S. C. R. 479.	Judgment reversed, but restored on further appeal.
McIntyre v. National Ins. Co. of Montreal (44 Q. B. 501).	5 A. R. 580.	Judgment affirmed.
McLean v. Dunn (39 Q. B. 551).	1 A. R. 153.	Judgment reversed.
McMaster v. King (42 Q. B. 409).	3 A. R. 106.	Judgment reversed.
Neill v. Union Mutual Life Ins. Co. (45 Q. B. 593).	7 A. R. 171.	Judgment affirmed.
Niagara High School Board, in re (39 Q. B. 362) 37 Q. B. 529.	1 A. R. 288.	Judgment affirmed.
Nickle v. Douglas (35 Q. B. 126).	37 Q. B. 51.	Judgment affirmed.
Norton v. Smith (20 Q. B. 213).	7 U. C. L. J. 263.	Judgment affirmed.
O'Connor v. Dunn (30 Q. B. 597).	2 A. R. 247.	Judgment reversed.
Ontario Salt Co. v. Larkin (35 Q. B. 229).	36 Q. B. 486.	Judgment affirmed.

CASE.	REPORT ON APPEAL.	RESULT OF APPEAL.
Parsons v. Citizens' Ins. Co. (43 Q. B. 261.) Parsons v. Queen Ins. Co. (43 Q. B. 271.)	4 A. R. 96 } aff. by Sup. 4 A. R. 103 } Ct. 4 S. C. R. 215, but reversed by Pr. Coun. 7 App. Cas. 96, except as to validity of Ont. Ins. Act.	Judgment affirmed, but reversed on further appeal.
Parsons v. Standard Ins. Co. (43 Q. B. 603).	4 A. R. 326; rev. by Sup. Ct. 5 S. C. R. 233.	Judgment reversed, but restored on further appeal.
Paterson v. Thompson (46 Q. B. 7).	9 A. R. 326.	Judgment reversed.
Queen, The, v. Frawley (46 Q. B. 153).	7 A. R. 246.	Judgment reversed.
Queen, The, v. Hodge (46 Q. B. 141).	7 A. R. 246 ; aff. by Pr. Coun. 9 App. Cas. 117	Judgment reversed.
Reg. v. Boucher (8 P. R. 20).	4 A. R. 191 *sub nom. In re* Boucher.	Judgment affirmed.
Rooney v. Lyon (40 Q. B. 366).	2 A. R. 53.	Judgment affirmed.
Royal Canadian Bank v. Carruthers (28 Q. B. 578).	29 Q. B. 283.	Judgment affirmed.
Royal Canadian Bank v. Miller (28 Q. B. 593).	29 Q. B. 266.	Judgment affirmed.
Scragg v. City of London (26 Q. B. 263).	28 Q. B. 457.	Judgment affirmed.
Sexton v. Paxton (21 Q. B. 389).	2 E. & A. 219.	Judgment affirmed.
Shannon v. Gore District mutual Ins. Co. (40 Q. B. 188).	2 A. R. 396.	Judgment reversed.
Shaw v. De Salaberry Nav. Co. (18 Q. B. 541).	6 U. C. L. J 197.	Judgment affirmed.
Sherboneau v. Beaver Mutual Ins. Co. (30 Q. B. 472).	33 Q. B. 1.	Judgment affirmed.
Smith v. Moffatt (27 Q. B. 195).	28 Q. B. 486.	Judgment affirmed.
Sowden v. Standard Fire Ins. Co. (44 Q. B. 95).	5 A. R. 290.	Judgment affirmed.
Sterling v. McEwan (17 Q. B. 361).	18 Q. B. 466.	Judgment reversed.
Superior & Savings Co. v. Lucas (44 Q. B. 106).	15 A. R. 748.	Judgment reversed.
Tench v. Great Western Ry. Co. (32 Q. B. 452).	33 Q. B. 8.	Judgment reversed.
Toms v. Township of Whitby (35 Q. B. 195).	37 Q. B. 100.	Judgment affirmed.
Toronto Street Ry. Co. v. Fleming (35 Q. B. 264).	37 Q. B. 116.	Judgment reversed.
Trust & Loan Co. v. Lawrason (45 Q. B. 176).	6 A. R. 286 ; aff. by Sup. Ct. 10 S. C. R. 679.	Judgment reversed.
Trust & Loan Co. v. Covert (32 Q. B. 222).	1 A. R. 26 ; rev. by Sup. Ct. 1 S. C. R. 564. *sub nom.* T. & L. Co. v. Ruttan.	Judgment reversed, but restored on further appeal.
Tylee v. Hinton (42 Q. B. 228).	3 A. R. 53.	Judgment affirmed.
Ulrich v. National Ins. Co. (42 Q. B. 141).	4 A. R. 84.	Judgment affirmed.
Van Velsor v. Hughson (45 Q. B. 252).	9 A. R. 390.	Judgment varied.

CASE.	REPORT ON APPEAL.	RESULT OF APPEAL.
Wallace v. Swift (28 Q. B. 563).	31 Q. B. 523.	Judgment reversed.
Warriner v. Kingsmill (8 Q. B. 407).	13 Q. B. 18.	Judgment affirmed.
Welland, County of, v. Buffalo & Lake Huron Ry. Co. (30 Q. B. 147).	31 Q. B. 539.	Judgment affirmed.
Whelan v. The Queen (28 Q. B. 2).	28 Q. B. 108.	Judgment affirmed on Error.
Widder v. Buffalo & Lake Huron Ry. Co. (24 Q. B. 520).	27 Q. B. 425.	Judgment affirmed.
Wilds v. Smith (41 Q. B. 136).	2 A. R. 8.	Judgment reversed.
Wilson v. Kerr (17 Q. B. 168).	18 Q. B. 470.	Judgment affirmed.
Wisconsin Bank v. Bank of British North America (21 Q. B. 284).	2 E. & A. 282.	Judgment affirmed.
Yeomans v. County of Wellington (43 Q. B. 522).	4 A. R. 301.	Judgment affirmed.

[25]

CASES IN THE ONTARIO COURT OF COMMON PLEAS CARRIED TO THE COURT OF APPEAL.

CASE.	REPORT ON APPEAL.	RESULT OF APPEAL.
Anchor Ins. Co. v. Phœnix Ins. Co. (30 C. P. 570).	6 A. R. 567.	Judgment affirmed.
Austin v. Dickson (11 C. P. 594).	2 E. & A. 373.	Judgment affirmed.
Bank of Toronto v. Eccles (10 C. P. 282).	2 E. & A. 53.	Judgment affirmed.
Banque Nationale v. Sparks (27 C. P. 320).	2 A. R. 112.	Judgment affirmed.
Barrie, Township of, v. Gillies (20 C. P. 369).	21 C. P. 213.	Judgment affirmed.
Berlin, Municipality of, v. Grange (5 C. P. 211).	1 E. & A. 279.	Judgment affirmed.
Birkett v. McGuire (31 C. P. 430).	7 A.R. 53 ; rev. by Sup. Ct. S. C. Dig. 598.	Judgment reversed, but restored on further appeal.
Boice v. O'Loane (28 C. P. 506).	3 A. R. 167.	Judgment reversed.
Boswell v. Sutherland (32 C. P. 131).	8 A. R. 233.	Judgment reversed.
Boys v. Smith (9 C. P. 27).	6 U. C. L. J. 182.	Judgment affirmed.
Braid v. Great Western Ry. Co. (10 C. P. 137).	7 U. C. L. J. 43 ; aff. by Pr. Coun. 1 Moo. N. S. 101.	Judgment affirmed.
Bullen v. Moodie (13 C. P. 126).	2 E. & A. 379 sub nom. Ponton v. Bullen.	Judgment affirmed.
Burnham v. Waddell (28 C. P. 263).	3 A. R. 288.	Judgment affirmed.
Cameron v. Wait (27 C. P. 475).	3 A. R. 175 ; aff. by Sup. Ct. S. C. Dig. 332.	Judgment affirmed.
Campbell v. Great Western Ry. Co. (20 C. P. 345).	20 C. P. 563.	Judgment affirmed.
Campbell v. Hill (22 C. P. 526).	23 C. P. 473.	Judgment affirmed.
Carlisle v. Tait (32 C. P. 43).	7 A. R. 10.	Judgment reversed.
Church v. Fenton (28 C. P. 384).	4 A. R. 159; aff. by Sup. Ct. 5 S. C. R. 239.	Judgment affirmed.
Cockburn v. Sylvester (27 C. P. 34).	1 A. R. 471.	Judgment reversed.
Coffey v. Quebec Bank (20 C. P. 110).	20 C. P. 555.	Judgment affirmed.
Coleman v. McDermott (5 C. P. 303).	1 E. & A. 445.	Judgment affirmed.
Commercial Bank of Canada v. Cotton (17 C. P. 214).	17 C. P. 447.	Judgment affirmed.
Contois v. Bonfield (25 C. P. 39).	27 C. P. 84.	Judgment affirmed.
Cruickshank and Corby in re (30 C. P. 466).	5 A. R. 415.	Judgment affirmed on equal division.

CASE.	REPORT ON APPEAL.	RESULT OF APPEAL.
Denmark v. McConaghy (29 C. P. 563).	None. Judgment on appeal aff. by Sup. Ct. 4 S. C. R. 609.	Judgment reversed.
Donly v. Holmwood (30 C. P. 240).	4 A. R. 555.	Judgment affirmed.
Doyle v. Bell (32 C. P. 632).	11 A. R. 326.	Judgment affirmed.
Fisher v. Jamieson (12 C. P. 601).	2 E. & A. 242.	Judgment affirmed.
Fitzgerald v. Grand Trunk Ry. Co. (28 C. P. 586).	4 A. R. 601 ; aff. by Sup. Ct. 5 S. C. R. 204.	Judgment affirmed.
Forsyth v. Galt (21 C. P. 408).	22 C. P. 115.	Judgment affirmed.
Fowler v. Vail (27 C. P. 417).	4 A. R. 267.	Judgment reversed.
Fulton v. Upper Canada Furniture Co. (32 C. P. 422).	9 A. R. 211.	Judgment reversed.
Gauhan v. St. Lawrance and Ottawa Ry. Co. (29 C. P. 102).	3 A. R. 392.	Judgment affirmed.
Gildersleeve v. McDougall (31 C. P. 164).	6 A. R. 553.	Judgment reversed.
Gotwalls v. Mulholland (15 C. P. 62).	3 E. & A. 194.	Judgment affirmed.
Graham v. Smith (27 C. P. 1).	Wiley v. Smith, 1 A. R. 179; aff. by Sup. Ct. 2 S. C. R. 1.	Decision overruled.
Grant & Great Western Ry. Co. (7 C. P. 438).	5 U. C. L. J. 210.	Judgment affirmed.
Haldan v. Kerr (12 C. P. 620).	2 E. & A. 382.	Judgment affirmed.
Hall, in re (32 C. P. 498).	8 A. R. 135.	Judgment affirmed.
Hamilton v. Holcomb (12 C. P. 38).	2 E. & A. 230.	Judgment affirmed.
Hamilton v. Myles (23 C. P. 293).	24 C. P. 309.	Judgment reversed.
Harold v. County of Simcoe (16 C. P. 43).	18 C. P. 1.	Judgment affirmed.
Hedstrom v. Toronto Car Wheel Co. (31 C. P. 475).	8 A. R. 627.	Judgment affirmed.
Hope v. White (17 C. P. 430).	19 C. P. 479.	Judgment affirmed.
Howell v. Alport (12 C. P. 375).	Wiley v. Smith, 1 A. R. 179; aff. by Sup. Ct. 2 S. C. R. 1.	Decision overruled.
Ianson v. Paxton (22 C. P. 505).	23 C. P. 439.	Judgment reversed.
Irwin v. City of Bradford (22 C. P. 18).	22 C. P. 421.	Judgment affirmed.
Lawrence v. Ketchum (28 C. P. 406).	4 A. R. 92.	Judgment affirmed.
Mason v. Agricultural Assur. Assoc. of Canada (16 C. P. 493).	18 C. P. 19.	Judgment reversed in part.
Mason (Assignee) v. Hamilton (22 C. P. 190).	22 C. P. 411.	Judgment reversed.
May v. Standard Ins. Co. (30 C. P. 51).	5 A. R. 605.	Judgment reversed.
Merchant's Bank v. Bostwick (28 C. P. 450).	3 A. R. 24.	Judgment affirmed.
Miller v. Reid (29 C. P. 576).	4 A. R. 479.	Judgment affirmed.
Mills v. Kerr (32 C. P. 68).	7 A. R. 769.	Judgment affirmed.

CASE.	REPORT ON APPEAL.	RESULT OF APPEAL.
Mills v. King (14 C. P. 223).	3 E. & A. 120.	Appeal quashed.
McArthur v. Town of Southwold (29 C. P. 216).	3 A. R. 295.	Judgment reversed.
McCrae v. Waterloo County Ins. Co. (26 C. P. 431).	1 A. R. 218.	Judgment affirmed.
McCulloch v. McIntee (13 C. P. 438).	2 E. & A. 390.	Judgment reversed.
McEdwards v. Palmer (28 C. P. 132).	2 A. R. 439.	Judgment reversed.
McGuffin v. Ryall (13 C. P. 115).	2 E. & A. 415.	Judgment reversed.
McKenzie v. Kittridge (24 C. P. 1, 145).	27 C. P. 65; aff. by Sup. Ct. 4 S. C. R. 368.	Judgment affirmed by equal division and on further appeal.
McKindsey v. Stewart (20 C. P. 295).	21 C. P. 226.	Judgment affirmed.
McLachlin v. Dixon (4 C. P. 71).	4 C. P. 307.	Judgment reversed.
McLaren v. Canada Central Ry. Co. (32 C. P. 324).	8 A. R. 564; aff. by Pr. Coun. 3 Can. Gaz. 346.	Judgment affirmed, by equal division and on further appeal.
McMaster v. Garland (31 C. P. 320).	8 A. R. 1.	Judgment affirmed.
McQueen v. Phœnix Mutual Insurance Co. (29 C. P. 511).	4 A. R. 289; rev. by Sup. Ct. 4 S. C. R. 660.	Judgment reversed, but restored on further appeal.
Neill v. Travellers' Ins. Co. (31 C. P. 394).	7 A. R. 570; aff. by Sup. Ct. 12 S. C. R. 55.	Judgment affirmed by equal division and on further appeal.
Niagara Election, *in re* (29 C. P. 261).	4 A. R. 407.	Appeal quashed.
Nicholls v. Cumming (25 C. P. 169).	26 C. P. 323; rev. by Sup. Ct. 1 S. C. R. 395.	Judgment reversed, but restored on further appeal.
Northern Ry. Co. v. Patton (15 C. P. 332).	2 L. J. N. S. 90.	Judgment affirmed.
Northwood v. Rennie (28 C. P. 202).	3 A. R. 37.	Judgment affirmed.
O'Connor v. Beatty (27 C. P. 203).	2 A. R. 497.	Judgment varied.
Oliver v. Grand Trunk Ry. Co. (28 C. P. 143).	Erb v. Grand Trunk Ry. Co. 3 A. R. 446.	Decision affirmed by equal division.
Oliver v. Newhouse (32 C. P. 90).	8 A. R. 122.	Judgment reversed.
Page v. Austin (30 C. P. 108).	7 A. R. 1; aff. by Sup. Ct. 10 S. C. R. 132.	Judgment reversed.
Palmer v. McLennan (22 C. P. 258).	22 C. P. 565.	Judgment affirmed.
Peek v. Shields (31 C. P. 112).	6 A. R. 639; aff. by Sup. Ct. 8 S. C. R. 579.	Judgment affirmed.
Pettigrew v. Doyle (17 C. P. 34).	17 C. P. 459.	Judgment affirmed.
Pim v. Municipal Council of Ontario (9 C. P. 302).	9 C. P. 304.	Judgment reversed.
Potter v. Carroll (9 C. P. 442).	1 E. & A. 341.	Judgment affirmed.
Provincial Insurance Co. v. Cameron (31 C. P. 523).	9 A. R. 56 *sub nom.* Provincial Ins. Co. v. Worts.	Judgment affirmed by equal division.
Queen, The, v. Town of Paris (12 C. P. 445).	9 U. C. L. J. 231.	Judgment affirmed.

CASE.	REPORT ON APPEAL.	RESULT OF APPEAL.
Quinlan v. Union Fire Ins. Co. (31 C. P. 618).	8 A. R. 376.	Judgment reversed.
Reg. v. Bishop of Huron (8 C. P. 253).	Mountjoy v. Reg. 1 E. & A. 429.	Decision affirmed.
Reg. v. Browne (31 C. P. 484).	6 A. R. 386.	Judgment affirmed.
Reg. v. Hunt (16 C. P. 145).	17 C. P. 443.	Judgment affirmed.
Reg. v. Law Society (20 C. P. 490).	21 C. P. 229.	Judgment affirmed.
Robins v. Victoria Mutual Fire Ins. Co. (31 C. P. 562).	6 A. R. 427.	Judgment affirmed.
Rooney v. Rooney (29 C. P. 347).	4 A. R. 255.	Judgment affirmed.
Rosenberger v. Grand Trunk Ry. Co. (32 C. P. 349).	8 A. R. 482 ; aff. by Sup. Ct. 9 S. C. R. 311.	Judgment affirmed.
Royal Canadian Bank v. Kelly (20 C. P. 519).	22 C. P. 279.	Judgment reversed.
Russell v. Canada Life Assur. Co. (32 C. P. 256).	8 A. R. 716.	Judgment affirmed.
Ryan v. Ryan (29 C. P. 449).	4 A. R. 563 ; rev. by Sup. Ct. 5 S. C. R. 387.	Judgment reversed, but restored on further app.
Samis v. Ireland (28 C. P. 478).	4 A. R. 118.	Judgment affirmed.
Samo v. Gore District Mutual Ins. Co. (26 C. P. 405).	1 A. R. 545 ; rev. by Sup. Ct. 2 S. C. R. 411.	Judgment reversed, but restored on further app.
Shannon v. Hastings Mutual Ins. Co. (26 C. P. 380).	2 A. R. 81 ; aff. by Sup. Ct. 2 S. C. R. 394.	Judgment affirmed.
Sheriff v. Holcombe (13 C. P. 590).	2 E. & A. 516.	Judgment affirmed.
Silsby v. Village of Dunnville (31 C. P. 301).	8 A. R. 524.	Judgment affirmed.
Stafford, Township of, v. Bell (31 C. P. 77).	6 A. R. 273.	Judgment reversed.
Stayner v. Applegarth (8 C. P. 133).	5 U. C. L. J. 210.	Judgment affirmed.
St. Catharines, Town of, v. Gardner (20 C. P. 107).	21 C. P. 190 *sub nom.* St. Catharines, etc., Road Co. v. Gardner.	Judgment affirmed.
Street v. County of Simcoe (12 C. P. 284).	2 E. & A. 211.	Judgment affirmed.
Supple v. Gilmour (5 C. P. 318).	None. Judg't on appeal aff. by Pr. Coun. 11 Moo. P. C. 551.	Judgment affirmed.
Sweeney v. President, etc., of Port Burwell Harbour (17 C. P. 574).	19 C. P. 376.	Judgment reversed.
Thorne v. Torrance (16 C. P. 445).	18 C. P. 29.	Judgment affirmed.
Todd v. London, Liverpool & Globe Ins. Co. (18 C. P. 192).	20 C. P. 523.	Judgment reversed.
Turley v. Benedict (31 C. P. 417).	7 A. R. 300.	Judgment reversed.
Victoria Mutual Fire Ins. Co. v. Thompson (32 C. P. 476).	9 A. R. 620.	Judgment affirmed.
Walton v. County of York (30 C. P. 217).	6 A. R. 181.	Judgment reversed.
Williamson v. Commercial Union Ins. Co. (25 C. P. 453).	26 C. P. 591.	Judgment reversed.
Wright v. Sun Mutual Life Ins. Co. (29 C. P. 221).	5 A. R. 218 ; aff. by Sup. Ct. 5 S. C. R. 466, *sub nom.* London Life Assur. Co. v. Wright.	Judgment affirmed.

CASES IN THE HIGH COURT OF JUSTICE FOR ONTARIO CARRIED TO THE COURT OF APPEAL.

CASE.	REPORT ON APPEAL.	RESULT OF APPEAL.
Abraham v. Abraham (19 O. R. 256).	18 A. R. 436.	Judgment affirmed.
Adams v. Watson Mfg. Co. (15 O. R. 218).	16 A. R. 2.	Judgment affirmed.
Aitcheson v. Mann (9 P. R. 253).	9 P. R. 473.	Judgment affirmed.
Alger v. Sarnia Oil Co., in re. (21 O. R. 440).	19 A. R. 446.	Judgment affirmed.
Allenby and Weir, in re. (13 P. R. 403).	14 P. R. 227.	Judgment affirmed.
Allison v. McDonald (23 O. R. 288).	20 A. R. 695.	Judgment reversed.
Anderson v. Canadian Pacific Ry. Co. (17 O. R. 747).	17 A. R. 480.	Judgment affirmed.
Anderson v. Fish (16 O. R. 476).	17 A. R. 28.	Judgment affirmed.
Archbold v. Building & Loan Assoc. (15 O. R. 237).	16 A. R. 1.	Judgment reversed.
Archer v. Severn (12 O. R. 615).	14 A. R. 723.	Judgment affirmed.
Ardill v. Citizens' Ins. Co. (22 O. R. 529).	20 A. R. 605.	Judgment affirmed.
Arscott v. Lilley { (11 O. R. 153). { (11 O. R. 285).	14 A. R. 297. 14 A. R. 283.	Judgment affirmed. Judgment reversed.
Atty.-Gen. v. Niagara Falls, etc., Tramway Co. (19 O. R. 624).	18 A. R. 453.	Judgment affirmed.
Atty.-Gen. v. Vaughan Road Co. 21 O. R. 507.	19 A. R. 234; rev. by Sup. Ct. 21 S.C.R.637.	Judgment reversed; restored on further appeal.
Atty.-Gen. of Canada v. Atty.-Gen. of Ontario (20 O. R. 222).	19 A. R. 31; appeal to Sup. Ct. stands for judgment.	Judgment affirmed.
Atty.-Gen. of Canada v. City of Toronto (20 O. R. 19).	18 A. R. 622; rev. by Sup. Ct. S. C. Dig. 57 and leave to appeal to Pr. Coun. refused.	Judgment affirmed, but reversed on further appeal.
Baker v. Atkinson (11 O. R. 735).	14 A. R. 409.	Judgment reversed.
Baldwin v. Kingstone (16 O. R. 341).	18 A. R. 63.	Judgment reversed.
Ball v. Crompton Corset Co. (9 O. R. 228).	12 A. R. 738.	Judgment affirmed.
Bank of Montreal v. Haffner (3 O. R. 183).	10 A. R. 592; aff. by Sup. Ct. S. C. Dig. 526, sub nom. Bank of Montreal v. Worswick.	Judgment affirmed.
Barber v. Clark (20 O. R. 522).	18 A. R. 435.	Judgment affirmed.
Barton, Township of, v. Hamilton (18 O. R. 199).	17 A. R. 346; aff. by Sup. Ct. 20 S. C. R. 173.	Judgment affirmed.

CASE.	REPORT ON APPEAL.	RESULT OF APPEAL.
Bate v. Canadian Pacific Ry. Co. (14 O. R. 625).	15 A. R. 388; rev. by Sup. Ct. 18 S. C. R. 697.	Judgment affirmed, but reversed on further appeal.
Beatty v. Neelon (9 O. R. 385).	12 A. R. 50; aff. by Sup. Ct. 13 S. C. R. 1.	Judgment reversed.
Beatty v. North-West Trans. Co. (6 O. R. 300).	11 A. R. 205; rev. by Sup. Ct. 12 S.C.R. 598; restored by Pr. Coun. 12 App. Cas. 589.	Judgment reversed.
Beatty v. Shaw (13 O. R. 21).	14 A. R. 600.	Judgment reversed.
Beaver v. Grand Trunk Ry. Co. (22 O. R. 667).	20 A. R. 476.	Judgment affirmed.
Beckett v. Grand Trunk Ry. Co. (8 O. R. 601).	13 A. R. 174; aff. by Sup. Ct. 16 S. C. R. 713.	Judgment affirmed by equal division.
Beemer v. Oliver (3 O. R. 523).	10 A. R. 656.	Judgment affirmed.
Beemer v. Village of Grimsby (8 O. R. 98).	13 A. R. 225.	Judgment affirmed.
Begg v. Ellison (11 C. L. T. 69).	14 P. R. 384.	Judgment reversed.
Bell v. Riddell (2 O. R. 25).	10 A. R. 544.	Judgment affirmed.
Bertram v. Massey Mfg. Co. (15 O. R. 516).	13 P. R. 184.	Judgment affirmed.
Betts v. Grand Trunk Ry. Co. (12 P. R. 86).	12 P. R. 634.	Judgment affirmed.
Betts v. Smith (15 A. R. 413).	16 A. R. 421.	Judgment reversed.
Bickford v. Town of Chatham (10 O. R. 257).	14 A. R. 32; aff. by Sup. Ct. 16 S. C. 235.	Judgment affirmed.
Blackley v. Kenney (19 O. R. 169).	18 A. R. 135.	Judgment reversed.
Bleakley v. Corporation of Prescott (7 O. R. 261).	12 A. R. 637.	Judgment reversed.
Bolt & Iron Co. in re. Livingstone's Case (14 O. R. 211).	16 A. R. 397.	Judgment affirmed.
Bond v. Conmee (15 O. R. 716).	16 A. R. 398; aff. by Sup. Ct. S. C. Dig. 511.	Judgment affirmed.
Brady v. Sadler (16 O. R. 49).	17 A. R. 365.	Judgment reversed.
Brayley v. Ellis (1 O. R. 119).	9 A. R. 565.	Judgment affirmed by equal division.
Brice v. Munro (7 O. R. 435).	12 A. R. 453.	Judgment reversed.
Brown v. Howland (9 O. R. 48).	15 A. R. 750.	Judgment affirmed.
Brown v. Moyer (23 O. R. 222).	20 A. R. 509.	Judgment reversed.
Bruce, Corporation of, v. McLay (3 O. R. 23).	11 A. R. 477.	Judgment affirmed.
Bull v. North British Canadian Investment Co. (14 O. R. 322).	15 A. R. 421.	Judgment affirmed.
Cain v. Junkin (6 O. R. 532).	13 A. R. 525.	Judgment affirmed.
Cameron v. Cusack (18 O. R. 520).	17 A. R. 489.	Judgment reversed.
Canada Atlantic Ry. Co. v. City of Ottawa (8 O. R. 201) 8 O. R. 183.	12 A. R. 234; aff. by Sup. Ct. 12 S. C. R. 365. Leave to appeal to Pr. Coun. granted, but not proceeded with.	Judgment affirmed.

CASE.	REPORT ON APPEAL.	RESULT OF APPEAL.
Canada Atlantic Ry. Co. v. Township of Cambridge (11 O. R. 392).	14 A. R. 299; aff. by Sup. Ct. 15 S. C. R. 219. Leave to appeal granted, but not proceeded with.	Judgment reversed.
Canada Cotton Co. v. Parmalee (13 P. R. 26).	13 P. R. 308.	Judgment reversed in part.
Canada Land Co. v. Municipality of Dysart (9 O. R. 495, 520).	12 A. R. 80.	Judgment affirmed.
Canada Temperance Act, *in re* (9 O. R. 154).	12 A. R. 677.	Judgment affirmed.
Canadian Locomotive Co. v. Copeland (14 O. R. 170).	16 A. R. 322.	Judgment reversed.
Carey v. City of Toronto (7 O. R. 194).	11 A. R. 416; aff. by Sup. Ct. 14 S. C. R. 172.	Judgment reversed.
Carter v. Grasset (11 O. R. 331).	14 A. R. 685.	Judgment reversed.
Central Bank of Canada, *in re*. Baines's Case (16 O. R. 293).	16 A. R. 237.	Judgment affirmed.
Central Bank, *in re* Nasmith's Case (16 O. R. 293).	18 A. R. 209.	Judgment affirmed.
Central Bank v. Garland (20 O. R. 142).	18 A. R. 438.	Judgment affirmed.
Chamberlen v. Clark (1 O. R. 135).	9 A. R. 273.	Judgment affirmed.
Charles, *in re*. Fulton v. Whatmough (1 O. R. 362).	10 A. R. 281.	Judgment reversed.
Clark and Township of Howard, *in re* (14 O. R. 598).	16 A. R. 72.	Judgment affirmed.
Clarkson v. Atty.-Gen. of Canada (15 O. R. 632).	16 A. R. 202.	Judgment affirmed.
Clarkson v. Sterling (14 O. R. 460).	15 A. R. 234.	Judgment affirmed.
Clayton v. McConnell (14 O. R. 608).	15 A. R. 560.	Judgment reversed.
Clouse v. Canada Southern Ry. Co. (4 O. R. 28).	11 A. R. 287 ; rev. by Sup. Ct. 13 S. C. R. 139.	Judgment affirmed ; reversed on further appeal.
Cochrane v. Boucher (3 O. R. 462).	8 A. R. 555.	Leave to appeal refused, there being no judgment to appeal from.
Cole v. Hall (12 P. R. 584).	13 P. R. 100.	Judgment affirmed.
Connolly v. Murrell (14 P. R. 187).	14 P. R. 270.	Judgment affirmed.
Conway v. Canadian Pacific Ry. Co. (7 O. R. 673).	12 A. R. 708.	Judgment affirmed.
Cosgrave Brewing & Malting Co. v. Starrs (5 O. R. 189).	11 A. R. 156 ; rev. by Sup. Ct. 12 S. C. R. 571.	Judgment affirmed ; reversed on further appeal.
Cottingham v. Cottingham (5 O. R. 704).	11 A. R. 624.	Judgment reversed.
Court v. Walsh (1 O. R. 167).	9 A. R. 294.	Judgment affirmed.
Coyne v. Broddy (13 O. R. 173).	15 A. R. 159.	Judgment reversed.
Crain v. Rapple (22 O. R. 519.	20 A. R. 291.	Judgment reversed.
Croft and Town of Peterboro', *in re* (17 O. R. 522).	17 A. R. 21.	Judgment affirmed.
Culverwell v. Birney (11 O. R. 265).	14 A. R. 266.	Judgment reversed.

CASE.	REPORT ON APPEAL.	RESULT OF APPEAL.
Cumberland v. Kearns (18 O. R. 151).	17 A. R. 281.	Judgment affirmed.
Cumming v. Landed Banking & Loan Co. (20 O. R. 382) 19 O. R. 426.	19 A. R. 447; rev. by Sup. Ct. 22 S. C. R. 246.	Judgment reversed, but restored on further appeal.
Dancey v. Grand Trunk Ry. Co. (20 O. R. 603).	19 A. R. 664.	Judgment varied.
Davis v. Lewis (8 O. R. 1).	23 C. L. J. 294.	Judgment affirmed.
Davies v. Gillard (21 O. R. 431).	19 A. R. 432.	Judgment reversed.
Doan v. Michigan Central Ry. Co. (18 O. R. 482).	17 A. R. 481.	Judgment reversed.
Dobell v. Ontario Bank and John Rochester (3 O. R. 299).	9 A. R. 484.	Judgment affirmed as to Rochester; reversed as to Ontario Bank.
Donovan v. Herbert (9 O. R. 89).	12 A. R. 298; aff. by Sup. Ct. S. C. Dig. 653.	Judgment affirmed.
Dorland v. Jones (7 O. R. 17).	12 A. R. 543; aff. by Sup. Ct. 14 S. C. R. 39.	Judgment reversed.
Douglas v. Hutchison (6 O. R. 581).	12 A. R. 110.	Judgment reversed.
Dover, Township of, v. Chatham (5 O. R. 325).	11 A. R. 248; aff. by Sup. Ct. 12 S. C. R. 321.	Judgment affirmed by equal division.
Duggan v. London & Canadian Loan Co. (19 O. R. 272).	18 A. R. 305; rev. by Sup. Ct. 20 S. C. R. 481, but restored by P. C. [1893] A. C. 506.	Judgment reversed.
Duncan v. Rogers (15 O. R. 699).	16 A. R. 3; reversed in part by Sup. Ct. 18 S. C. R. 710.	Judgment reversed.
Dunlop v. Dunlop (6 O. R. 141).	10 A. R. 670.	Judgment reversed.
Duncan v. Tees (11 P. R. 66).	11 P. R. 296.	Judgment varied.
Dyment v. Thomson (9 O. R. 566).	12 A. R. 659; aff. by Sup. Ct. 13 S. C. R. 303.	Judgment affirmed.
Eastman v. Bank of Montreal (10 O. R. 79).	23 C. L. J. 235.	Judgment affirmed by equal division.
Eberts v. Brooke (10 P. R. 257).	11 P. R. 296.	Judgment reversed.
Edgar v. Northern Ry. Co. (4 O. R. 201).	11 A. R. 452.	Judgment affirmed.
Edmonds v. Hamilton Provident & Loan Soc. (19 O. R. 677).	18 A. R. 347.	Judgment reversed in part.
Electric Despatch Co. of Toronto v. Bell Telephone Co. (17 O, R. 495).	17 A. R. 292; aff. by Sup. Ct. 20 S. C. R. 83.	Judgment affirmed by equal division.
Elliott v. Brown (2 O. R. 352).	11 A. R. 228.	Judgment reversed.
Erdman v. Town of Walkerton (22 O. R. 693).	20 A. R. 444.	Judgment affirmed.
Faulds v. Harper (2 O. R. 405).	9 A. R. 537; rev. by Sup. Ct. 11 S. C. R. 639.	Judgment reversed; restored on further appeal.
Finch v. Gilray (16 O. R. 303).	16 A. R. 484.	Judgment reversed.
Fleming, in re (11 P. R. 272).	11 P. R. 426.	Judgment reversed.
Fleming v. City of Toronto (20 O. R. 547).	19 A. R. 318.	Judgment affirmed.
Forbes v. Michigan Central Ry. Co. (22 O. R. 568).	20 A. R. 584.	Judgment affirmed.
Fox v. Symington (9 O. R. 767).	13 A. R. 296.	Judgment reversed.

CASE.	REPORT ON APPEAL.	RESULT OF APPEAL.
Freidrich v. Freidrich (10 P. R. 308).	10 P. R. 546.	Judgment varied on re-hearing.
Friendly v. Needles (10 P. R. 267).	10 P. R. 427.	Judgment affirmed.
Gage v. Canada Pub. Co. (6 O. R. 68).	11 A. R. 403; aff. by Sup. Ct. 11 S. C. R. 306.	Judgment affirmed.
Gibbons v. McDonald (19 O. R. 290).	18 A. R. 159; aff. by Sup. Ct. 20 S. C. R. 587.	Judgment affirmed.
Gibbons v. Wilson (17 O. R. 290).	17 A. R. 1.	Judgment affirmed.
Godson and City of Toronto, *in re* (16 O. R. 275).	16 A. R. 452; aff. by Sup. Ct. 18 S. C. R. 36.	Judgment reversed.
Goldsmith v. City of London (11 O. R. 26).	23 C. L. J. 294; rev. by Sup. Ct. 16 S. C. R. 231.	Judgment affirmed by equal division; reversed on further appeal.
Gooderham v. City of Toronto (21 O. R. 120).	19 A. R. 641.	Judgment affirmed.
Gould v. Hope (21 O. R. 624).	20 A. R. 247.	Judgment reversed.
Grant v. Carnock (16 O. R. 406].	16 A. R. 532.	Judgment affirmed.
Gray v. Town of Dundas (11 O. R. 317).	13 A. R. 588.	Judgment affirmed.
Green v. Corporation of Orford (15 O. R. 506).	16 A. R. 4.	Judgment reversed.
Green v. Watson (2 O. R. 627).	10 A. R. 113.	Judgment affirmed by equal division.
Hager v. O'Neill (21 O. R. 27).	20 A. R. 198.	Judgment affirmed.
Hall v. Farquharson (13 O. R. 593).	15 A. R. 457.	Judgment affirmed.
Hall v. Hall (20 O. R. 684) 20 O. R. 168.	19 A. R. 292.	Judgment affirmed.
Hall Mfg. Co. v. Hazlett (8 O. R. 465).	11 A. R. 749.	Judgment affirmed.
Hamilton v. Groesbeck (19 O. R. 76).	18 A. R. 437.	Judgment affirmed.
Hamilton Provident & Loan Soc. v. Campbell (5 O. R. 371).	12 A. R 250.	Judgment affirmed.
Hands v. Law Society of Upper Canada (17 O. R. 300) 16 O. R. 625.	17 A. R. 41.	Judgment reversed.
Harvey v. Grand Trunk Ry. Co. (9 P. R. 80).	7 A. R. 715.	Judgment affirmed.
Harvey and Town of Parkdale, *in re* (16 O. R. 372).	16 A. R. 468.	Judgment affirmed.
Hately v. Merchants' Despatch Transportation Co. (4 O. R. 723). (11 P. R. 9).	12 A. R. 201; aff. by Sup. Ct. 14 S. C. R. 572. 12 A. R. 640.	Judgment affirmed. Judgment reversed.
Hayes v. Elmsley (21 O. R. 562).	19 A. R. 291; rev. by Sup. Ct.	Judgment affirmed, but reversed on further appeal.
Heaslip v. Heaslip (14 P. R. 21).	14 P. R. 165.	Judgment affirmed.
Henderson v. Bank of Hamilton (23 O. R. 327).	20 A. R. 646.	Judgment reversed.
Henderson v. Killey (14 O. R. 137).	17 A. R. 456; rev. by Sup. Ct. 18 S. C. R. 698, *sub nom.* Osborne v. Henderson.	Judgment affirmed by equal division, and reversed on further appeal.
Hendrie v. Neelon (3 O. R. 603).	12 A. R. 41.	Judgment affirmed.
Hilliard v. Arthur (10 P. R. 281).	10 P. R. 426.	Judgment affirmed.

CASE.	REPORT ON APPEAL.	RESULT OF APPEAL.
Hislop v. Township of McGillivray (12 O. R. 749).	15 A. R. 687; aff. by Sup. Ct. 17 S. C. R. 479.	Judgment affirmed.
Hobbs v. Guardian Assur. Co. (7 O. R. 634). Hobbs v. Northern Ins. Co. (8 O. R. 343).	11 A. R. 741; rev. by Sup. Ct. 12 S. C. R. 631.	Judgment in both cases affirmed, but reversed on further appeal.
Hogaboom v. Cox (15 P. R. 23).	15 P. R. 127.	Judgment reversed.
Holliday v. Hogan (22 O. R. 235).	20 A. R. 29S.	Judgment reversed.
Hollinger v. Canadian Pacific Ry. Co. (21 O. R. 705).	20 A. R. 244.	Judgment affirmed.
Howes v. Dominion Fire & Marine Ins. Co. (2 O. R. 89).	8 A. R. 644.	Judgment reversed.
Huggins v. Law (11 O. R. 565).	14 A. R. 383.	Judgment reversed.
Humphrey v. Archibald (21 O. R. 553).	20 A. R. 267.	Judgment reversed.
Huntington v. Attrill (17 O. R. 245).	18 A. R. 136 ; rev. by Pr. Coun.[1893] A. C. 150.	Judgment affirmed, but reversed on further appeal.
Hutchinson v. Canadian Pacific Ry. Co. (17 O. R. 347).	16 A. R. 429.	Judgment affirmed.
Hyatt v. Mills (20 O. R. 351).	19 A. R. 329.	Judgment reversed.
International Wrecking Co. v. Lobb (11 O. R. 408).	12 P. R. 207.	Appeal quashed, being deemed abandoned by proceedings.
Jack v. Jack (10 O. R. 1).	12 A. R. 476.	Judgment affirmed.
James v. Ontario & Quebec Ry. Co. (12 O. R. 624).	15 A. R. 1.	Judgment affirmed.
Jarrard, in re (4 O. R. 265).	20 C. L. J. 145.	Judgment affirmed.
Johnston v. Oliver (3 O. R. 26).	None; aff. by Sup. Ct. S. C. Dig. 651.	Judgment affirmed.
Jordan v. Dunn (13 O. R. 267).	15 A. R. 744.	Judgment affirmed.
Kent v. Kent (20 O. R. 445).	19 A. R. 352.	Judgment affirmed.
Klœpfer v. Gardner (10 O. R. 415).	14 A. R. 60; aff. by Sup. Ct. 15 S. C. R. 390.	Judgment reversed.
Knight v. Medora (11 O. R. 138).	14 A. R. 112.	Judgment affirmed.
Lawson v. McGeoch (22 O. R. 474).	20 A. R. 464.	Judgment affirmed.
Leach v. Grank Trunk Ry. Co. (13 P. R. 388).	13 P. R. 467.	Judgment reversed.
Lee v. MacMahon (2 O. R. 654).	11 A. R. 555.	Judgment affirmed.
Leeds & Grenville v. Brockville (17 O. R. 261).	18 A. R. 548.	Judgment reversed.
Leitch v. Grand Trunk Ry. Co. (12 P. R. 671) 12 P. R. 541.	13 P. R. 369.	Judgment affirmed by equal division.
Lemay v. Canadian Pacific Ry. Co. (18 O. R. 314).	17 A. R. 293.	Judgment affirmed.
Lemay v. McRae (16 O. R. 307).	16 A. R. 348; aff. by Sup. Ct. 18 S. C. R. 280.	Judgment affirmed.
Lemesurier v. Macaulay (22 O. R. 316).	20 A. R. 421.	Judgment affirmed.

CASE.	REPORT ON APPEAL.	RESULT OF APPEAL.
Lett v. St. Lawrence & Ottawa Ry. Co. (1 O. R. 545).	11 A. R. 1; aff. by Sup. C. 11 S. C. R. 422, and leave to appeal to Pr. Coun. refused.	Judgment reversed.
Lilley & Allin, *in re* (21 O. R. 424).	19 A. R. 101.	Judgment affirmed.
London & Canadian Loan Co. v. Morphy (10 O. R. 86).	14 A. R. 577.	Judgment affirmed.
London Mutual Ins. Co. v. City of London (11 O. R. 592).	15 A. R. 629.	Judgment affirmed.
Long v. Hancock (7 O. R. 154).	12 A. R. 137 ; rev. by Sup. Ct. 12 S. C. R. 532.	Judgment affirmed by equal division, and reversed on further appeal.
Long Point Co. v. Anderson (19 O. R. 487).	18 A. R. 401.	Judgment reversed.
Lowson v. Canadian Farmers' Co. (9 P. R. 185).	8 A. R. 613.	Judgment reversed.
Macdonnell v. Robinson (8 O. R. 53).	12 A. R. 270.	Judgment affirmed.
Maclennan v. Gray (16 O. R. 321).	16 A. R. 224 ; rev. by Sup. Ct. 18 S. C. R. 553 *sub nom.* Gray v. Coughlin.	Judgment reversed, but restored on further appeal.
Magee v. Gilmore (17 O. R. 620).	17 A. R. 27; aff. by Sup. Ct. 18 S. C. R. 579.	Judgment affirmed.
Magurn v. Magurn (3 O. R. 570).	11 A. R. 178.	Judgment affirmed
Maritime Bank v. Stewart (13 P. R. 262) 13 P. R. 86.	13 P. R. 491; appeal to Sup. Ct. quashed.	Judgment affirmed.
Marsh v. Webb (21 O. R. 281).	19 A. R. 564 ; aff. by Sup. Ct.	Judgment affirmed.
Marshall v. McRae (16 O. R. 495).	17 A. R. 139 ; rev. by Sup. Ct. 19 S.C.R.10.	Judgment affirmed ; reversed on further appeal.
Martin v. Magee (19 O. R. 705).	18 A. R. 384.	Judgment reversed.
Martin v. McAlpine (3 O. R. 499).	8 A. R. 675.	Judgment reversed.
Martin v. McMullen (20 O. R. 257) 19 O. R. 230.	18 A. R. 559.	Judgment reversed.
Masse v. Masse (10 P. R. 574).	11 P. R. 81.	Judgment reversed.
Massey Mfg. Co. *in re* (11 O. R. 444).	13 A. R. 446.	Judgment affirmed.
Matthews v. Hamilton Powder Co. (12 O. R. 58).	14 A. R. 261.	Judgment reversed.
Marthinson v. Patterson (20 O. R. 720) 20 O. R. 125).	19 A. R. 188.	Judgment affirmed.
Mendellshon Co. v. Graham (19 O. R. 83).	17 A. R. 378.	Judgment affirmed.
Merchants' Bank v. Lucas (13 O. R. 520).	15 A. R. 573; aff. by Sup. Ct. 18 S. C. R. 704.	Judgment reversed.
Midland Railway Co. v. Ontario Rolling Mills Co. (2 O. R. 1).	10 A. R. 677.	Judgment affirmed.
Miller v. Brown (3 O. R. 210).	9 P. R. 542.	Leave to appeal refused, notice not given in time.
Miller v. Confederation Life Ins. Co. (11 O. R. 120).	14 A. R. 218; aff. by Sup. Ct. 14 S. C. R. 330.	Judgment affirmed.
Mingeaud v. Packer (21 O. R. 267).	19 A. R. 290.	Judgment affirmed by equal division.
Mitchell v. Gormley (9 O. R. 139).	14 A. R. 55.	Judgment affirmed.

CASE.	REPORT ON APPEAL.	RESULT OF APPEAL.
Mitchell v. City of London Assur. Co. (12 O. R. 706).	15 A. R. 262.	Judgment affirmed.
Moffatt v. Scratch (8 O. R. 147) 6 O. R. 564.	12 A. R. 157.	Judgment affirmed.
Monteith v. Merchants' Despatch Transportation Co. (1 O. R. 47).	9 A. R. 282.	Judgment affirmed.
Moorehouse v. Bostwick (5 O. R. 104).	11 A. R. 76.	Judgment reversed.
Morton v. Hamilton Provident & Loan Soc. (10 P. R. 636).	11 P. R. 82.	Judgment affirmed.
Moses v. Moses (13 P. R. 12).	13 P. R. 144.	Judgment affirmed.
Moxley v. Canada Atlantic Ry. Co. (10 P. R. 553).	11 P. R. 39.	Judgment reversed.
MacDonald v. Crombie (2 O. R. 243).	10 A. R. 92; aff. by Sup. Ct. 11 S. C. R. 107.	Judgment affirmed.
MacDonnell v. Blake (17 O. R. 104).	17 A. R. 312.	Judgment affirmed.
MacDonnell v. Robinson (8 O. R. 53).	12 A. R. 270.	Judgment affirmed.
MacDougall, *in re* (13 O. R. 204).	15 A. R. 150 ; rev. by Sup. Ct. 18 S. C. R. 203.	Judgment affirmed, but reversed on further appeal.
McArthur v. Northern & Pacific Junction Ry. Co. (15 O. R. 733).	17 A. R. 86.	Judgment affirmed by equal division.
McCarthy v. Cooper (8 O. R. 316).	12 A. R. 284.	Judgment affirmed.
McCraney v. McCool (19 O. R. 470).	18 A. R. 217.	Judgment affirmed.
MacDonald v. Field (9 P. R. 220).	12 P. R. 213.	Judgment reversed.
McDonald v. Murray (2 O. R. 573).	11 A. R. 101.	Judgment reversed.
McDonald v. McCall (9 O. R. 185).	12 A. R. 593; aff. by Sup. Ct. 13 S. C. R. 247.	Judgment affirmed.
McGeachie v. North American Life Assur. Co. (22 O. R. 151).	20 A. R. 187.	Judgment reversed.
McGibbon v. Northern Ry. Co. (11 O. R. 307).	14 A. R. 91.	Judgment reversed.
McGregor v. Norton (13 P. R. 28).	13 P. R. 223.	Judgment reversed.
McGugan v. McGugan (21 O. R. 289).	19 A. R. 56; aff. by Sup. Ct. 21 S. C. R. 267.	Judgment reversed.
McKay v. Magee (13 P. R. 106).	13 P. R. 146.	Judgment affirmed.
McKenzie v. Dwight (2 O. R. 366).	11 A. R. 381.	Judgment affirmed by equal division.
McLaren v. Commercial Union Assur. Co. (7 O. R. 64).	12 A. R. 279.	Judgment affirmed.
McLean v. Brown (15 O. R. 313).	16 A. R. 106.	Judgment affirmed by equal division.
McLean v. Clark (21 O. R. 683).	20 A. R. 660.	Judgment reversed in part.
McMichael v. Wilkie (19 O. R. 739).	18 A. R. 548.	Judgment reversed.
McMillan v. Grand Trunk Ry. Co. (12 O. R. 103).	15 A. R. 14; rev. by Sup. Ct. 16 S. C. R. 543, and leave to appeal to Pr. Coun. refused.	Judgment affirmed, but reversed on further appeal.
McNeeley v. Williams (9 O. R. 728).	13 A. R. 324.	Judgment reversed.

CASE.	REPORT ON APPEAL.	RESULT OF APPEAL.
McRae and Ontario & Quebec Ry. Co., *in re* (12 P. R. 282).	12 P. R. 327.	Judgment affirmed.
New Hamburg v. County of Waterloo (22 O. R. 193).	20 A. R. 1 ; rev. by Sup. Ct. 22 S. C. R. 296.	Judgment affirmed by equal division; reversed on further appeal.
Niagara Grape Co. v. Nellis (13 P. R. 179).	13 P. R. 258.	Leave to appeal refused.
Oakville, Corporation of, *in re* (9 O. R. 274).	12 A. R. 225.	Judgment reversed.
Oakwood High School Board, *in re* (15 O. R. 686).	16 A. R. 87 *sub nom. Re* Oakwood and Township of Mariposa.	Judgment reversed.
O'Brien v. Clarkson (2 O. R. 525).	10 A. R. 603.	Judgment affirmed.
O'Donohoe, *in re* { (12 P. R. 612).	14 P. R. 317; aff. by Sup. Ct. 10 S. C. R. 356.	Judgment affirmed by equal division.
(14 P. R. 571).	15 P. R. 93.	Judgment affirmed.
O'Donohoe v. Whitby (2 O. R. 424).	20 C. L. J. 146.	Judgment affirmed.
O'Meara v. City of Ottawa (11 O. R. 603).	15 A. R. 75 ; aff. by Sup. Ct. 14 S. C. R. 742.	Judgment affirmed.
Ontario & Quebec Ry. Co. v. Philbrick (5 O. R. 674).	None ; aff. by Sup. Ct. 12 S. C. R. 288.	Judgment affirmed.
Ontario Loan & Debenture Co. v. Hobbs (15 O. R. 440).	16 A. R. 255; rev. by Sup. Ct. 18 S. C. R. 483.	Judgment reversed ; restored on further appeal.
Ontario Natural Gas Co. v. Gosfield (19 O. R. 591).	18 A. R. 626.	Judgment affirmed.
Ostrom and Township of Sidney, *in re* (15 O. R. 43).	15 A. R. 372.	Judgment reversed.
Owen Sound S. S. Co. v. Canadian Pacific Ry. Co. (17 O. R. 691).	17 A. R. 482.	Judgment affirmed.
Paisley v. Wills (19 O. R. 303).	18 A. R. 210.	Judgment affirmed.
Parkes v. St. George (2 O. R. 342).	10 A. R. 496.	Judgment reversed.
Partlo v. Todd (12 O. R. 171).	14 A. R. 444; aff. by Sup. Ct. 17 S. C. R. 196.	Judgment affirmed.
Peterboro' Real Estate Co. v. Patterson (13 O. R. 142).	15 A. R. 751.	Judgment varied.
Petrie v. Guelph Lumber Co. (2 O. R. 218).	11 A. R. 336; aff. by Sup. Ct. 11 S. C. R. 450.	Judgment affirmed.
Petrie v. Hunter (2 O. R. 233).	10 A. R. 127.	Judgment affirmed.
Phipps, *in re* (1 O. R. 585).	19 C. L. J. 110.	Judgment affirmed.
Pierce v. Palmer (12 P. R. 275).	12 P. R. 308.	Appeal not entertained.
Plumb v. Steinhoff (2 O. R. 614).	11 A. R. 788; aff. by Sup. Ct. 14 S. C. R. 739.	Judgment reversed.
Potts v. Boivine (16 O. R. 152).	16 A. R. 191.	Judgment affirmed.
Powell v. Peck } (12 O. R. 492). Peck v. Powell }	15 A. R. 138.	{ Judgment in both cases affirmed.
Pratt v. City of Stratford (14 O. R. 260).	16 A. R. 5.	Judgment affirmed.
Pryce and City of Toronto, *in re* (16 O. R. 726).	20 A. R. 16.	Judgment affirmed.
Ratte v. Booth (11 O. R. 491) 10 O. R. 351.	14 A. R. 419.	Judgment affirmed.
Reddick v. Saugeen Mutual Insur. Co. (14 O. R. 596).	15 A. R. 363.	Judgment affirmed.

CASE.	REPORT ON APPEAL.	RESULT OF APPEAL.
Reg. v. County of Wellington (17 O. R. 615).	17 A. R. 421; aff. by Sup. Ct. *sub nom.* Quirt v. The Queen, 19 S. C. R. 510.	Judgment affirmed.
Reg. v. Elborne (21 O. R. 504).	19 A. R. 439.	Judgment reversed.
Reg. v. Eli (10 O. R. 727).	13 A. R. 526.	Appeal quashed.
Reg. v. Hazen (23 O. R. 387).	20 A. R. 633.	Judgment reversed.
Reg. v. Howland (11 O. R. 633).	14 A. R. 184 ; rev. by Sup. Ct. *sub nom. Re* O'Brien,16 S.C.R. 197	Judgment affirmed, reversed on further appeal.
Reg. v. St. Catharines' Milling Co. (10 O. R. 196).	13 A. R. 148; aff. by Sup. Ct. 13 S. C. R. 577, and by Pr. Coun. 14 App. Cas. 46.	Judgment affirmed.
Reg. v. Wason (17 O. R. 58).	17 A. R. 221.	Judgment reversed.
Reid v. Murphy (12 P. R. 246).	12 P. R. 338.	Judgment reversed.
Ringrose v. Ringrose (10 P. R. 299).	10 P. R. 596.	Judgment affirmed.
Roberts v. Donovan (21 O. R. 535).	30 C. L. J. 33. *sub nom.* Berry v. Donovan.	Judgment affirmed.
Robertson and North Easthope, *in re* (15 O. R. 423).	16 A. R. 214.	Judgment reversed.
Robinson v. Harris (21 O. R. 43.	19 A.R.134; rev. by Sup. Ct. 21 S. C. R. 390.	Judgment affirmed by equal division, but reversed on further appeal.
Rogers v. Wilson (12 P. R. 322).	12 P. R. 545.	Judgment affirmed.
Ross v. Edwards (14 P. R. 523).	15 P. R. 150.	Judgment reversed.
Ryan v. Bank of Montreal (12 O. R. 39).	14 A. R. 533.	Judgment affirmed on equal division.
Ryan v. Cooley (14 O. R. 13).	15 A. R. 379.	Judgment varied.
Saderquist v. Ontario Bank (14 O. R. 586).	15 A. R. 609.	Judgment affirmed.
Sawyer v. Pringle (20 O. R. 111).	18 A. R. 218.	Judgment affirmed.
Saylor v. Cooper (2 O. R. 398).	8 A. R. 707.	Judgment affirmed.
Scott v. Corporation of Tilsonburgh (10 O. R. 119).	13 A. R. 233.	Judgment affirmed.
Scott v. Crerar (11 O. R. 541).	14 A. R. 152.	Judgment reversed.
Scott v. Niagara Navigation Co. (15 P. R. 400).	30 C. L. J. 37.	Judgment affirmed.
Scribner v. McLaren (2 O. R. 265).	12 A. R. 367 *sub nom.* Scribner v. Kinloch ; aff. by Sup. Ct. 14 S. C. R. 77.	Judgment affirmed by equal division and on further appeal.
Seymour v. Lynch (7 O. R. 471).	14 A. R. 738; aff. by Sup. Ct. 15 S. C. R. 341.	Judgment affirmed by equal division.
Sheard v. Laird (15 O. R. 533).	15 A. R. 339.	Judgment reversed.
Sibbald v. Grand Trunk Ry. Co. Tremayne v. Grand Trunk Ry. Co. (19 O. R. 164).	18 A. R. 184; aff. by Sup. Ct. 20 S. C. R. 259.	Judgment affirmed.

CASE.	REPORT ON APPEAL.	RESULT OF APPEAL.
Sievewright v. Leys (1 O. R. 375).	20 C. L. J. 145.	Judgment affirmed.
Sinden v. Brown (17 O. R. 706).	17 A. R. 173.	Judgment affirmed.
Skinner, *in re* (13 P. R. 276).	13 P. R. 447.	Judgment affirmed.
Smart, *in re*. (12 P. R. 435) 12 P. R. 312.	12 P. R. 635.	Judgment affirmed, and appeal to Supreme Ct. quashed.
Smith v. Fleming (12 P. R. 520).	12 P. R. 657.	Judgment affirmed.
Smith v. London Ins. Co. (11 O. R. 38).	14 A. R. 328.	Judgment affirmed.
Smith v. Millions (15 O. R. 453).	16 A. R. 140.	Judgment reversed.
Smith v. McLellan (11 O. R. 191).	15 A. R. 738 *sub nom.* Smith v. Chishome.	Judgment affirmed.
Smith v. Port Dover & Lake Huron Ry. Co. (8 O. R. 256).	12 A. R. 288.	Judgment affirmed.
Standard Fire Ins. Co., *in re*. Barber's Case, Copp, Clark & Co.'s Case (7 O. R. 448).	12 A. R. 486.	Judgment reversed.
Standard Fire Ins. Co. *in re*. Caston's Case (7 O. R. 448).	12 A. R. 466.	Judgment affirmed.
Standard Fire Insurance Co. *in re*. Kelly's Case (7 O. R. 204).	12 A. R. 486.	Judgment reversed.
St. Denis v. Baxter (13 O. R. 41).	15 A. R. 387.	Judgment reversed.
Stevens v. Barfoot (9 O. R. 692).	13 A. R. 366.	Judgment reversed in part.
Stevenson v. Davis (21 O. R. 642).	19 A. R. 591; rev. by Sup. Ct.	Judgment affirmed, but reversed on further appeal.
Stillwell v. Rennie (7 O. R. 355).	11 A. R. 724.	Judgment reversed.
St. Vincent v. Greenfield (12 O. R. 297).	15 A. R.-567.	Judgment affirmed.
Sutherland v. Cox (6 O. R. 505).	15 A. R. 541; aff. by Sup. Ct. S. C. Dig. 9.	Judgment affirmed.
Temperance Colonization Co. v. Evans (12 P. R. 48).	12 P. R. 380.	Judgment affirmed.
Temperance Colonization Co. v. Fairfield (16 O. R. 544).	17 A. R. 205.	Judgment affirmed.
Thames Navigation Co. v. Reid (9 O. R. 754).	13 A. R. 303.	Judgment reversed.
Thompson v. Hay (22 O. R. 583).	20 A. R. 379.	Judgment affirmed.
Thompson v. Robinson (15 O. R. 662).	16 A. R. 175.	Judgment reversed in part.
Thorold, Town of, v. Neelon (20 O. R. 86).	18 A. R. 658 ; rev. by Sup. Ct. 22 S. C. R. 390.	Judgment reversed in part, but restored on further appeal.
Todd v. Dun Wiman & Co. (12 O. R. 791).	15 A. R. 85.	Judgment reversed.
Tomlinson v. Northern Ry. Co. (11 P. R. 419).	11 P. R. 526.	Appeal not entertained.
Toronto and Toronto Street Ry. Co., *in re* (22 O. R. 374).	20 A. R. 125; aff. by Pr. Coun. [1893] A. C. 511.	Judgment affirmed.
Travis v. Travis (8 O. R. 516).	12 A. R. 438.	Judgment affirmed.
Trinity College v. Hill (2 O. R. 348).	10 A. R. 99.	Judgment reversed.

CASE.	REPORT ON APPEAL.	RESULT OF APPEAL.
Trust & Loan Co. v. Stevenson (21 O. R. 571).	20 A. R. 66.	Judgment reversed.
Union Fire Ins. Co., *in re* (10 O. R. 489).	13 A. R. 268; rev. by Sup. Ct. 14 S. C. R. 624.	Judgment affirmed, but reversed on further appeal.
VanKoughnet v. Denison (1 O. R. 349).	11 A. R. 699.	Judgment varied.
Vansickle v. Vansickle (1 O. R. 107).	9 A. R. 352.	Judgment reversed.
Vickers' Express Co. v. Canadian Pacific Ry. Co. (9 O. R. 251).	13 A. R. 210.	Judgment affirmed.
Victoria, County of, v. County of Peterboro' (15 O. R. 446).	15 A. R. 617; aff. by Sup. Ct. S. C. Dig. 558.	Judgment reversed.
Vogel v. Grand Trunk Ry. Co. Morton v. Grand Trunk Ry. Co. (2 O. R. 197).	10 A. R. 162; aff. by Sup. Ct. 11 S. C. R. 612.	Judgment affirmed by equal division and on further appeal.
Waldie and Village of Burlington *in re* (7 O. R. 192).	13 A. R. 104.	Judgment affirmed.
Warin v. London & Canadian Loan Co. (7 O. R. 706).	12 A. R. 327; aff. by Sup. Ct. 14 S. C. R. 232.	Judgment affirmed.
Warnock v. Kloepfer (14 O. R. 288).	15 A. R. 324; aff. by Sup. Ct. 18 S. C. R. 701.	Judgment affirmed.
Waterous v. Town of Palmerston (20 O. R. 411).	19 A. R. 47; aff. by Sup. Ct. 21 S. C. R. 556.	Judgment affirmed.
Weegar v. Grand Trunk Ry. Co. 23 O. R. 436).	20 A. R. 528.	Judgment affirmed.
Wells v. Lindop (14 O. R. 275) 13 O. R. 431.	15 A. R. 695.	Judgment affirmed.
West v. Parkdale. Carroll v. Parkdale (8 O. R. 59) 7 O. R. 270.	12 A. R. 393; rev. by Sup. Ct. 12 S. C. R. 250, and by Pr. Coun. 12 App. Cas. 602.	Judgment reversed, but restored on further appeal.
Western Assur. Co. v. Ontario Coal Co. (20 O. R. 595) 19 O. R. 462.	19 A. R. 41; aff. by Sup. Ct. 21 S. C. R. 383.	Judgment affirmed.
Western Canada Loan & Savings Co. v. Dunn (9 P. R. 490).	9 P. R. 587.	Judgment reversed.
White v. Township of Gosfield (2 O. R. 237).	10 A. R. 555.	Judgment affirmed.
Whiting v. Honey (9 O. R. 314). {	12 A. R. 119.	Motion to quash appeal refused.
	13 A. R. 7; aff. by Sup. Ct. 14 S. C. R. 515.	Judgment reversed.
Wicksteed v. Munro (10 O. R. 283).	13 A. R. 486.	Judgment affirmed.
Wilkins v. McLean (10 O. R. 58).	13 A. R. 467; rev. by Sup. Ct. 11 S.C.R. 22.	Judgment reversed, but restored on further appeal.
York, County of, v. Toronto Gravel Co. (3 O. R. 584).	11 A. R. 675; aff. by Sup. Ct. 12 S. C. R. 517.	Judgment affirmed by equal division.
Yost v. Adams (8 O. R. 411).	13 A. R. 129.	Judgment affirmed.
Young v. Midland Ry. Co. (16 O. R. 738).	19 A. R. 265; aff. by Sup. Ct. 22 S. C. R. 190.	Judgment affirmed.
Young v. Saylor (23 O. R. 513).	20 A. R. 645.	Judgment affirmed.
Zimmer v. Grand Trunk Ry. Co. (21 O. R. 628).	19 A. R. 693.	Judgment affirmed.
Zoological Society of Ontario, *in re* Cox's Case (17 O. R. 331).	16 A. R. 543.	Judgment reversed.

CASES IN THE COURTS OF LOWER CANADA AND QUEBEC CARRIED TO THE PRIVY COUNCIL.

Case.	Report on Appeal.	Result of Appeal.
Abbott v. McGibbon (28 L. C. J. 120, 7 L. N. 179) 5 L. N. 431.	10 App. Cas. 653 ; 54 L. J. 39 ; 54 L. T. 138.	Judgment affirmed.
Allan v. Pratt (M. L. R. 3 Q. B. 7).	13 App. Cas. 780 ; 57 L. J. 104 ; 59 L. T. 674 ; 15 Q. L. R. 18 ; 32 L. C. J. 278.	Leave to appeal refused.
Allan v. Quebec Warehouse Co.	12 App. Cas. 101 ; 56 L. J. 6 ; 56 L. T. 30.	Judgment affirmed.
Angers, Atty.-Gen. v. Murray, 3 L. N. 108 ; 25 L. C. J. 208.	3 L. N. 308.	Leave to appeal refused by Court of Queen's Bench.
Angers, Atty.-Gen. of Quebec v. Queen Ins. Co. (1 L. N. 3) 7 R. L. 545 ; 21 L. C. J. 77.	3 App. Cas. 1090 ; 38 L. T. 897 ; 22 L. C. J. 307.	Judgment affirmed.
Atkinson v. Usborne.	Wheeler P. C. Law 34.	Judgment reversed.
Bank of British North America v. Cuvillier (4 L. C. J. 241) 2 L. C. J. 154.	14 Moo. P. C. 187 ; 4 L. T. 159.	Judgment reversed.
Bank of Montreal v. Simson (5 L. C. J. 169) 10 L. C. R. 225).	14 Moo. P. C. 417 ; 5 L. T. 70 ; 8 Jur. N. S. 246 ; 6 L. C. J. 1 ; 11 L. C. R. 377.	Judgment affirmed.
Bank of Toronto v. European Assur. Soc. (14 L. C. J. 186) 13 L. C. J. 63.	7 R. L. 57.	Judgment affirmed.
Bank of Upper Canada v. Bradshaw.	L. R. 1. P. C. 479 ; 4 Moo. N. S. 406.	Judgment affirmed.
Banque d'Hochelaga v. Murray.	15 App. Cas. 414 ; 59 L. J. 102 ; 63 L. T. 63.	Judgment affirmed.
Banque Jacques Cartier v. Banque d'Epargne de Montreal (M. L. R. 2 Q. B. 64).	13 App. Cas. 111 ; 57 L. J. 42.	Judgment reversed.
Bartley v. Bartley.	Ramsay's App. Cas. 56. Wheeler's P. C. Law 74.	Leave to appeal granted by Ct. of Queen's Bench. Judgment affirmed.
Beaudry v. Mayor of Montreal.	11 Moo. P. C. 399 ; 6 W. R. 346.	Judgment reversed.
Bedard, in re.	7 Moo. P. C. 23.	Precedence refused to petitioner by Court of Queen's Bench granted by Pr. Coun.
Bell v. Corporation of Quebec, 2 Q. L. R. 305.	5 App. Cas. 84 ; 49 L. J. 1 ; 41 L. T. 451.	Judgment affirmed.
Belleville v. Doucet (1 Q. L. R. 250).	1 Q. L. R. 283.	Leave to appeal refused by Ct. of Queen's Bench.
Bellingham v. Freer.	1 Moo. P. C. 333.	Judgment affirmed.
Boston v. Lelievre (14 L. C. R. 457).	L. R. 3 P. C. 157 ; 6 Moo. N. S. 427 ; 39 L. J. 17 ; L. T. 735 ; 18 W. R. 408.	Judgment affirmed.

CASE.	REPORT ON APPEAL.	RESULT OF APPEAL.
Boswell v. Kilborn. Boswell v. Kilborn. Boswell v. Kilborn.	12 Moo. P. C. 467. 13 Moo. P. C. 476. 15 Moo. P. C. 309; 6 L. T. 79; 8 Jur. N. S.443; 10 W. R. 517; 6 L. C. J. 108; 12 L. C. R. 161.	Leave to appeal granted. Further security ordered. Judgment reversed, and new trial ordered.
Brewster v. Lamb.	3 L. N. 75.	Leave to appeal granted by Ct. of Queen's Bench.
Brook v. Bloomfield (6 R. L. 533).	Ramsay's App. Cas. 54.	Leave to appeal refused by Court of Queen's Bench.
Brown v. Cure, etc., de Notre Dame de Montreal (17 L. C. J. 89).	L. R. 6 P. C. 157; 44 L. J. 1; 31 L. T. 555; 23 W. R. 184; 20 L. C. J. 228.	Judgment reversed.
Brown v. Gugy (11 L. C. R. 401).	2 Moo. N. S. 341 ; 10 L. T. 45; 10 Jur. N. S. 525; 12 W. R. 493; 14 L. C. R. 213.	Judgment affirmed.
Brown v. Mayor of Montreal (18 L. C. J. 146) 16 L. C. J. 1 ; 4 R. L. 7.	2 App. Cas. 168; 35 L. T. 870.	Judgment affirmed.
Browning v. Provincial Ins. Co.	L. R. 5 P. C. 263 ; 28 L. T. 853 ; 21 W. R. 587.	Judgment reversed.
Bryant v. Banque de Peuple. ⎰ Q. R. 1 S. Bryant v. Quebec Bank. ⎱ C. 53.	[1893] A. C. 170 ; 9 Times L. R. 322.	Judgment affirmed.
Buntin v. Hibbard (1 L. C. L. J. 34).	1 L. C. L. J. 60.	Leave to appeal granted by Ct. of Queen's Bench.
Burstall v. Baptist.	21 W. R. 485.	Judgment reversed.
Cantin v. Hochelaga Bank (32 L. C. J. 22).	10 Can. Gaz. 586.	Leave to appeal refused.
Chapman v. Lancashire Assur. Co., 13 L. C. J. 36.	7 R. L. 47.	Judgment affirmed.
Chaudiere Gold Mining Co. v. Desbarats (15 L. C. J. 44) 13 L. C. J. 182.	L. R. 5 P. C. 277 ; 42 L. J. 73 ; 29 L. T. 377 ; 21 W. R. 935 ; 17 L. C. J. 275; 4 R. L. 645.	Judgment affirmed.
Chevrotiero v. City of Montreal (6 L. N. 348).	12 App. Cas. 149 ; 56 L. J. 1 ; 56 L. T. 3.	Judgment affirmed.
Connecticut Fire Ins. Co. v. Kavanagh (M. L. R. 7 Q. B. 323) M. L. R. 5 S.C. 262).	[1892] A. C. 473 ; 8 Times L. R. 752.	Judgment affirmed.
Cure de Vercheres v. Corporation of Ver- cheres (4 R. L. 87).	L. R. 6 P. C. 330 ; 44 L. J. 34 ; 32 L. T. 178 ; 23 W. R. 712 ; 19 L. C. J. 141.	Judgment affirmed.
Cushing v. Dupuy (22 L. C. J. 201).	5 App. Cas. 409 ; 42 L. T. 445; 3 L. N. 171 ; 24 L. C. J. 151.	Judgment affirmed.
Cuvillier v. Aylwin.	2 Knapp 72 ; Stu. L. C. R. 527.	Leave to appeal refused.
Dallimore v. Brooke.	Ramsay's App. Cas. 54.	Leave to appeal granted by Ct. of Queen's Bench.
Dansereau, *Ex parte* (19 L. C. J. 210).	Ramsay's App. Cas. 55.	Leave to appeal refused by Ct. of Queen's Bench.
Darling v. Templeton (19 L. C. J. 85).	19 L. C. J. 105.	Leave to appeal refused by Ct. of Q. B. judg- ment not being final.
De-Gaspe v. Bessener.	4 App. Cas. 135 ; 48 L. J. 1 ; 39 L. T. 550.	Judgment affirmed.
Dobie v. Temporalities Board (3 L. N. 244, 250) 2 L. N. 277 ; 23 L. C. J. 71.	7 App. Cas. 136 ; 51 L. J. 46 ; 46 L. T. 1 ; 26 L. C. J. 170.	Judgment reversed.

CASE.	REPORT ON APPEAL.	RESULT OF APPEAL.
Donegani v. Donegani Stu. L. C. R. 460.	3 Knapp 63 ; Stu. L. C. R. 605.	Judgment affirmed.
Dorion v. St. Sulpice.	5 App. Cas. 362 ; 49 L. J. 32 ; 42 L. T. 132.	Judgment affirmed.
Dufaux v. Herse (17 L. C. R. 246).	L. R. 4 P. C. 468 ; 9 Moo. N. S. 281 ; 42 L. J. 1 ; 21 W. R. 313 ; 17 L. C. J. 147.	Judgment affirmed.
Durocher v. Beaubien.	Stu. L. C. R. 307.	Judgment affirmed.
Eliza Keith, The (Cook V. A. R. 107).	Wheeler P. C. Law 52.	Judgment affirmed.
Ermatinger v. Gugy.	5 Moo. P. C. 1.	Judgment reversed.
Evanturel v. Evanturel, 14 L. C. R. 151.	L. R. 2 P. C. 462 ; 6 Moo. N. S. 75 ; 38 L. J. 41 ; 21 L. T. 4 ; 17 W. R. 541 ; 1 Q. L. R. 144.	Judgment affirmed.
Evanturel v. Evanturel (16 L. C. J. 258) 16 L. C. R. 353.	L. R. 6 P. C. 1 ; 43 L. J. 58 ; 31 L. T. 105 ; 23 W. R. 32 ; 1 Q. L. R. 74 ; 5 R. L. 606.	Judgment reversed.
Fraser v. Abbott, 15 L. C. J. 147.	L. R. 6 P. C. 96 ; 44 L. J. 26 ; 31 L. T. 596 ; 23 W. R. 422 ; 20 L. C. J. 197 ; 6 R. L. 365.	Judgment reversed.
Frechette v. Compagine Manufacturiere de St. Hyacinthe (5 L. N. 187 ; 1 Dor. Q. B. 378).	9 App. Cas. 170 ; 53 L. J. 20 ; 50 L. T. 62 ; 28 L. C. J. 202.	Judgment reversed.
Gibb v. Beacon Fire & Life Ins. Co. 10 L. C. R. 402.	1 Moo. N. S. 73 ; 7 L. T. 574 ; 9 Jur. N. S. 185 ; 11 W. R. 194.	Judgment reversed.
Gilmour v. Paradis (M. L. R. 3 Q. B. 449 ; 31 L. C. J. 232).	14 App. Cas. 645 ; 59 L. J. 38 ; 61 L. T. 442 *sub nom.* Gilmour v. Mauroit, 33 L. C. J. 231.	Judgment affirmed.
Goldring v. Banque d'Hochelaga (2 L. N. 230).	5 App. Cas. 371 ; 49 L. J. 82.	Order for leave to appeal rescinded.
Grant v. Etna Ins. Co. (5 L. C. J. 285 ; 11 L. C. R. 330) 11 L. C. R. 128.	15 Moo. P. C. 516 ; 6 L. T. 735 ; 8 Jur. N. S. 705 ; 10 W. R. 772.	Judgment reversed.
Gravel v. Martin (Ramsay's App. Cas. 285).	22 L. C. J. 272 ; Ramsay's App. Cas. 956.	Judgment affirmed.
Gugy v. Brown.	L. R. 1 P. C. 411 ; 4 Moo. N. S. 315 ; 36 L. J. 38 ; 15 W. R. 721 ; 11 L. C. J. 141 ; 14 L. C. R. 213.	Judgment reversed.
Herrick v. Sixby (8 L. C. J. 324).	L. R. 1 P. C. 436 ; 4 Moo. N. S. 349 ; 11 L. C. J. 129.	Judgment reversed.
Hibernian, The (2 Stu. V. A. 148).	L. R. 4 P. C. 511 ; 27 L. T. 725 ; 1 Q. L. R. 319.	Judgment affirmed.
Hutchinson v. Gillespie.	2 Moo. P. C. 243.	Reference to take accounts ordered.
Hutchinson v. Gillespie.	4 Moo. P. C. 378.	Commission refused.
Jette v. McNaughton (20 L. C. J. 255) 19 L. C. J. 153.	21 L. C. J. 192.	Security on appeal approved by Ct. of Q. B.

CASE.	REPORT ON APPEAL.	RESULT OF APPEAL.
Johnson v. Connolly.	16 L. C. J. 100.	New security on appeal ordered.
Jones v. Lemoine.	2 L. C. L. J. 161; 17 L. C. R. 377.	Execution refused where appeal to Pr. Coun. had been lodged.
Jones v. Stanstead, etc. Ry. Co., 17 L. C. R. 81.	L. R. 4 P. C. 98; 8 Moo. N. S. 312; 41 L. J. 19; 26 L. T. 456; 20 W. R. 417; 16 L. C. J. 157.	Judgment affirmed.
Kershaw v. Kirkpatrick.	3 App. Cas. 345; 22 L. C. J. 92.	Judgment affirmed.
Kierkowski v. Dorion (2 L. C. L. J. 69).	L. R. 2 P. C. 291; 5 Moo. N. S. 397; 38 L. J. 12; 20 L. T. 170; 14 L. C. J. 20.	Judgment affirmed.
King v. Pinsonneault.	L. R. 6 P. C. 245; 44 L. J. 42; 32 L. T. 174; 33 W. R. 576; 22 L. C. J. 58.	Judgment reversed.
King v. Tunstall, 14 L. C. J. 197.	L. R. 6 P. C. 55; 31 L. T. 564; 23 W. R. 365; 20 L. C. J. 49; 6 R. L. 358.	Judgment affirmed.
Labrador Co. v. The Queen.	[1893] A. C. 104; 16 L. N. 67.	Judgment affirmed.
Lacroix v. Moreau (1 L. C. L. J. 33; 15 L. C. R. 485).	16 L. C. R. 180.	Leave to appeal from interlocutory judgment refused by Ct. of Q. B.
Lake St. Clair v. Underwriters (Cook, V. A. Rep. 43).	2 App Cas. 389 *sub nom.* Wilson v. Canada Shipping Co.; 36 L.T. 155, 3 Asp. N. S. 361.	Judgment reversed.
Lambkin v. South-Eastern Ry. Co.	22 L. C. J. 21.	Leave to appeal refused by Ct. of Queen's Bench.
	21 L. C. J. 325; 1 L. N. 55.	Special leave granted by Privy Council.
	5 App. Cas. 352; 28 W. R. 837; 3 L. N. 162.	Judgment reversed.
Lareau v. Dunn (7 L. N. 218).	57 L. J. 108; 32 L. C. J. 227.	Judgment reversed.
Leclerc v. Beaudry, 10 L. C. J. 20.	L. R. 5 P. C. 362; 29 L. T. 410; 21 W. R. 487; 17 L. C. J. 178; 5 R. L. 626.	Judgment reversed.
Leduc v. Provincial Ins. Co. 14 L. C. J. 273.	L. R. 6 P. C. 224; 43 L. J. 49; 31 L. T. 142; 22 W. R. 929; 19 L. C. J. 281.	Judgment affirmed.
Lemoine v. Lionais, 2 L. C. L. J. 163.	6 R. L. 123.	Judgment affirmed.
Logan v. Le Mesurier.	6 Moo. P. C. 116.	Judgment varied.
Loranger, Atty.-Gen. v. Colonial Building Assoc.	9 App.Cas. 157; 53 L.J. 27; 49 L. T. 789; 7 L. N. 10; 27 L. C. J. 295.	Judgment reversed.
Lord v. Elliott (27 L. C. J. 30; 5 L. N. 124; 2 Dor. Q. B. 337).	52 L. J. 23; 48 L. T. 542; Ramsay's App. Cas. 937.	Judgment reversed.
L'Union St. Jacques de Montreal v. Belisle, 15 L. C. J. 212.	L. R. 6 P. C. 31; 31 L. T. 111; 22 W. R. 933; 20 L. C. J. 29.	Judgment reversed.

CASE.	REPORT ON APPEAL.	RESULT OF APPEAL.
Lussier v. Hochelaga	3 L. N. 209.	Leave to appeal refused by Court of Queen's Bench.
Macfarlane v. Leclaire.	15 Moo. P. C. 181 ; 8 Jur. N. S. 267 ; 6 L. C. J. 370.	Motion to rescind order for leave to appeal refused.
	1 Moo. N. S. 1 ; 12 L. C. R. 374.	Judgment reversed.
Malo v. Migneault (14 L. C. J. 141).	L. R. 4 P. C. 123 ; 8 Moo. N. S. 347 ; 41 L. J. 11 : 26 L. T. 329 ; 20 W. R. 527 ; 16 L. C. J. 289 ; 3 R. L. 606.	Judgment reversed.
Marois, *in re.*	15 Moo. P. C. 189 ; 8 Jur. N. S. 268 ; 10 W. R. 326.	Special leave to appeal granted.
Martin v. Lee (9 L. C. R. 376).	14 Moo. P. C. 142 ; 4 L. T. 657 ; 9 W. R. 522 ; 14 L. C. R. 84.	Judgment reversed.
Meiklejohn v. Atty.-Gen. of Quebec.	2 Knapp. 328 ; Stu. L. C. R. 581.	Judgment affirmed.
Middlemiss v. Les Seurs Dames Hospitallie de St. Joseph (1 L. N. 51).	3 App. Cas. 1102 ; 47 L. J. 89 ; 38 L. T. 899 ; 22 L. C. J. 149.	Judgment affirmed.
Miner v. Gilmour.	12 Moo. P. C. 131 ; 7 W. R. 328 ; 9 L. C. R. 115.	Judgment affirmed.
Molson v. Carter (3 L. N. 258 ; 25 L. C. J. 63).	Ramsay's App. Cas. 1014.	Leave to appeal refused by Court of Queen's Bench.
Molson v. Carter (26 L. C. J. 159). (6 L. N. 372 ; 3 Dor. Q. B. 279).	8 App. Cas. 530 ; 52 L. J. 46 ; 49 L. T. 83.	Judgment affirmed.
	10 App. Cas. 664.	Judgment affirmed.
Montreal, City of, v. Devlin.	1 L. N. 151 ; 22 L. C. J. 136.	Leave to appeal granted by Court of Queen's Bench.
Montreal, Mayor, etc., of, v. Drummond (18 L. C. J. 225).	1 App. Cas. 384 ; 45 L. J. 33 ; 35 L. T. 106 ; 22 L. C. J. 1.	Judgment reversed.
Montreal, Mayor of, v. Hubert.	21 L. C. J. 85.	Leave to appeal granted by Court of Queen's Bench after expiry of time to apply.
Montreal Assur. Co. v. McGillivray. (2 L. C. J. 221 ; 8 L. C. R. 401).	13 Moo. P. C. 87 ; 8 W. R. 165 ; 9 L. C. R. 488.	Judgment reversed,
	13 Moo. P. C. 125 ; 9 W. R. 370.	Venire de novo ordered.
Montreal, etc., Ry. Co. v. Bourgoin (23 L. C. J. 96).	5 App. Cas. 381 : 49 L. J. 68 ; 42 L. T. 414 ; 3 L. N. 185 ; 24 L. C. J. 193.	Judgment reversed in part.
Moore v. Harris.	1 App. Cas. 318 ; 45 L. J. 55 ; 34 L. T. 519 ; 24 W. R. 887 ; 2 Q. L. R. 147 ; 3 Asp. N. S. 173.	Judgment affirmed.
Morrison v. City of Montreal.	3 App. Cas. 148 ; 47 L. J. 21.	Judgment affirmed.
Motz v. Moreau (7 L. C. R. 147).	13 Moo. P. C. 376 ; 8 W. R. 395 ; 10 L. C. R. 84.	Judgment affirmed.
	13 Moo. P. C. 396 ; 9 W. R. 421.	Application for re-hearing refused.

CASE.	REPORT ON APPEAL.	RESULT OF APPEAL.
Muir v. Muir (15 L. C. J. 309).	L. R. 5 P. C. 66 ; 43 L. J. 7 ; 30 L. T. 205 ; 22 W. R. 268 ; 18 L. C. J. 96.	Judgment affirmed.
Mullin v. Archambault (3 L. C. L. J. 90).	3 L. C. L. J. 117.	Leave to appeal refused by Ct. of Q. B. ; application too late.
MacLaren v. Murphy. } Connolly v. McLaren. }	L. R. 4 P. C. 262 ; 8 Moo. N. S. 1 ; 21 W. R. 8.	Judgment reversed.
McCarthy v. Judah.	12 Moo. P. C. 47.	Judgment reversed.
McConnell v. Murphy.	L. R. 5 P. C. 203 ; 28 L. T. 713.	Judgment reversed.
McDonald v. Joly (2 L. N. 2 ; 10 R. L. 391) 1 L. N. 446.	2 L. N. 104.	Leave to appeal granted by Ct. of Queen's Bench.
McDonald v. Lambe (9 L. C. J. 281).	L. R. 1 P. C. 539 ; 4 Moo. N. S. 486 ; 36 L. J. 70 : 11 L. C. J. 335 : 17 L. C. R. 293 ; 4 L. C. L. J. 8.	Judgment affirmed.
McDougall v. McGreevy (14 Q. L. R. 30). {	11 Can. Gaz. 394.	Motion to rescind order granting leave to appeal refused.
	13 Can. Gaz. 396.	Judgment reversed.
McGreevy v. Russell (14 R. L. 348).	56 L. T. 501.	Judgment affirmed.
McKay v. Rutherford.	6 Moo. P. C. 413.	Judgment affirmed.
McLeod v. Masham.	4 L. N. 99.	Leave to appeal refused by Ct. of Queen's Bench.
Nault v. Price (11 Q. L. R. 309 ; 4 Dor. Q. B. 348).	12 App. Cas. 110 ; 56 L. J. 29 ; 13 Q. L. R. 286.	Judgment affirmed.
Norina, The (1 Q. L. R. 211).	3 Asp. N. S. 272.	Judgment affirmed.
Normanton, The (Cook V. A. Rep. 65 ; 2 Q. L. R. 134).	Cook, V. A. Rep. 75n.	Leave to appeal granted, but appeal abandoned.
North British & Mercantile Ins. Co. v. Lambe (M. L. R. 1 Q. B. 122) ; M. L. R. 1 S. C. 32.	12 App. Cas. 575 ; 56 L. J. 87 ; 57 L. T. 377 ; 13 Q. L. R. 196 ; 32 L. C. J. 1 *sub nom.* Bank of Toronto v. Lambe.	Judgment affirmed.
Nye v. McDonald, 2 L. C. J. 159.	L. R. 3 P. C. 331 ; 7 Moo. N. S. 134 ; 39 L. J. 34 ; 23 L. T. 220 ; 18 W. R. 1075.	Judgment affirmed.
*O'Farrell v. Brassard (1 L. N. 25) 3 Q. L. R. 33).	1 L. N. 115 ; 4 Q. L. R. 214.	Leave to appeal refused by Ct. of Queen's Bench.
Pacaud v. Gagne (17 L. C. R. 357).	17 L. C. R. 375.	Leave to appeal in case of *quo warranto* refused by Ct. of Queen's Bench.
Pacaud v. Queen Ins. Co, (21 L. C. J. 111).	2 Steph. Dig. 70.	Leave to appeal refused by Ct. of Queen's Bench.
Pacaud v. Rickaby (1 Q. L. R. 245).	Ramsay's App. Cas. 54.	Leave to appeal granted by Ct. of Queen's Bench.
Pacaud v. Roy.	16 L. C. R. 398.	Leave to appeal refused by Ct. of Queen's Bench.
Panet v. Hamel.	2 App. Cas. 121 ; 46 L. J. 5 ; 35 L. T. 741 ; 3 Q. L. R. 173.	Judgment reversed.
Pollok v. Bradbury.	8 Moo. P. C. 227.	Judgment reversed.

CASE.	REPORT ON APPEAL.	RESULT OF APPEAL.
Prentice v. McDougall (28 L. C. J. 169 ; 7 L. N. 162 ; 4 Dor. Q. B. 91).	8 L. N. 153 ; Ramsay's App. Cas. 996.	Judgment affirmed.
Prevost v. Compagnie de Fives Lille (4 Dor. Q. B. 33).	11 App. Cas. 643 ; 54 L. J. 34 ; 54 L. T. 97 ; 8 L. N. 297 ; 29 L. C. J. 268.	Judgment reversed.
Quebec, The (Cook V. A. Rep. 32).	Wheeler P. C. Law 18.	Judgment affirmed.
Quebec & Richmond Ry. Co. v. Quinn (6 L. C. R. 129, 350).	12 Moo. P. C. 232.	Judgment affirmed.
Quebec Fire Ins. Co. v. Anderson.	{ 7 L. C. J. 150. / 13 Moo. P. C. 477.	Leave to appeal granted. Order granting leave rescinded.
Quebec Fire Ins. Co. v. St. Louis.	7 Moo. P. C. 286.	Judgment reversed.
Quebec Marine Ins. Co. v. Commercial Bank of Canada (13 L. C. J. 267).	L. R. 3 P. C. 234 ; 7 Moo. N. S. 1 ; 39 L. J. 53 ; 22 L. T. 559 ; 18 W. R. 769.	Judgment reversed.
Queen, The, v. Coote.	L. R. 4 P. C. 599 ; 9 Moo. N. S. 463 ; 42 L. J. 45 ; 29 L. T. 111 ; 18 L. C. J. 103.	Judgment reversed.
Queen, The, v. Ramsay (11 L. C. J. 152).	L. R. 3 P. C. 427 ; 7 Moo. N. S. 263 ; 15 L. C. J. 17.	Judgment reversed.
Redfield v. Corporation of Wickham.	13 App. Cas. 467 ; 57 L. J. 94 ; 58 L. T. 455 ; 4 Times L. R. 317 ; 11 L. N. 113 ; 33 L. C. J. 170.	Judgment affirmed.
Reg. v. Exchange Bank of Canada (M. L. R. 1 Q. B. 302) 29 L. C. J. 117.	11 App. Cas. 157 ; 55 L. J. 5 ; 54 L. T. 802 ; 2 Times L. R. 342 ; 30 L. C. J. 194.	Judgment reversed.
Renaud v. Tourangeau (13 L. C. R. 278).	L. R. 2 P. C. 4 ; 5 Moo. N. S. 5 ; 37 L. J. 1 ; 17 L. C. R. 451.	Judgment reversed.
Renny v. Moat (2 L. N. 97).	4 L. N. 195.	Judgment affirmed.
Reynar v. Porteous (11 Q. L. R. 297).	13 App. Cas. 120 ; 57 L. J. 28 ; 57 L. T. 891 ; 32 L. C. J. 55.	Judgment reversed.
Rogerson v. Reid.	1 Knapp 362 ; Stu. L. C. R. 412.	Judgment reversed.
Rolland v. Cassidy (M. L. R. 2 Q. B. 238) 7 L. N. 70.	13 App. Cas. 770 ; 57 L. J. 99 ; 59 L. T. 873 ; 32 L. C. J. 169.	Judgment affirmed.
Ryland v. DeLisle (12 L. C. J. 29).	L. R. 3 P. C. 17 ; 6 Moo. N. S. 225 ; 38 L. J. 67 ; 21 L. T. 325 ; 14 L. C. J. 12.	Judgment reversed.
Savageau v. Gauthier (1 Rev. Crit. 248).	L. R. 5 P. C. 494 ; 22 W. R. 667 ; 5 R. L. 602.	Appeal dismissed, unless petition for special leave lodged before a date named, case not being appealable as of right.
Scott v. Pacquet (4 L. C. J. 149).	L. R. 1 P. C. 552 ; 4 Moo. N. S. 505 ; 36 L. J. 65.	Judgment affirmed.
Senecal v. Hatton (M. L. R. 1 Q. B. 112) 6 L. N. 220.	8 Can. Gaz. 251.	Judgment affirmed.

CASE.	REPORT ON APPEAL.	RESULT OF APPEAL.
Senecal v. Panze (M. L. R. 5 Q. B. 461) M. L. R. 1 S. C. 465 ; 7 L. N. 30.	14 App. Cas. 637.	Judgment affirmed.
Shaw v. Jeffrey.	13 Moo. P. C. 432 ; 3 L. T. 1 ; 10 L. C. R. 340.	Judgment affirmed.
Simard v. Townsend.	6 L. C. R. 147.	Leave to appeal refused by Ct. of Queen's Bench.
Singleton v. Knight (14 Q. L. R. 39) ; 13 Q. L. R. 70.	13 App. Cas. 788 ; 57 L. J. 106 ; 59 L. T. 738 ; 14 Q. L. R. 257.	Judgment affirmed.
Smith v. Brown.	2 Moo. P. C. 35.	Judgment reversed.
Smith v. St. Lawrence Tow Boat Co.	L. R. 5 P. C. 308 ; 28 L. T. 885 ; 21 W. R. 569.	Judgment affirmed.
Stanton v. Home Fire Ins. Co. (2 L. N. 238) ; 21 L. C. J. 211.	2 L. N. 314.	Leave to appeal refused by Ct. of Queen's Bench.
Stephens v. Mayor of Montreal.	3 App. Cas. 605 ; 47 L. J. 67.	Judgment affirmed.
St. Louis v. St. Louis (Stu. L. C. R. 575).	1 Moo. P. C. 143.	Motion to dismiss appeal for delay refused.
	3 Moo. P. C. 398.	Judgment affirmed.
Symes v. Cuvillier (1 L. N. 302).	5 App. Cas. 138 ; 49 L. J. 54 ; 42 L. T. 198.	Judgment affirmed.
Theberge v. Landry.	2 App. Cas. 102 ; 46 L. J. 1 ; 35 L. T. 640 ; 25 W. R. 216 ; 3 Q. L R. 202.	Leave to appeal refused.
Tobin v. Murison.	5 Moo. P. C. 110.	Judgment affirmed as to account stated. Venire de Novo ordered as to damages.
Torrance v. Bank of British North America (15 L. C. J. 169) ; 12 L. C. J. 325.	L. R. 5 P. C. 246 ; 29 L. T. 109 ; 21 W. R. 529 ; 17 L. C. J. 185.	Judgment affirmed.
Trigge v. Lavallee.	15 Moo. P. C. 270 ; 8 L. T. 154 ; 9 Jur. N. S. 261 ; 11 W. R. 404 ; 7 L. C. J. 85 ; 13 L. C. R. 132.	Judgment reversed.
Voyer v. Richer, 13 L. C. J. 213.	L. R. 5 P. C. 461 ; 30 L. T. 506 ; 22 W. R. 849 ; 5 R. L. 591.	Judgment affirmed.
Wardle v. Bethune (12 L. C. J. 321).	L. R. 4 P. C. 33 ; 8 Moo. N. S. 223 ; 41 L. J. 1 ; 26 L. T. 81 ; 20 W. R. 374 ; 16 L. C. J. 85.	Judgment affirmed.
Whitfield v. Macdonald (26 L. C. J. 69 ; 2 Dor. Q. B. 157).	8 App. Cas. 733 ; 52 L. J. 70 ; 49 L. T. 446 ; 32 W. R. 730 ; 6 L. N. 278 ; 27 L. C. J. 165.	Judgment reversed.
Whyte v. Home Ins. Co.	19 L. C. J. 196.	Motion to have appeal declared deserted refused by Ct. of Queen's Bench.
Whyte v. Western Assurance Co.	22 L. C. J. 215 ; 7 R. L. 106.	Judgment affirmed.
Young v. Dental Association (2 L. N. 292).	2 L. N. 294.	Leave to appeal from Court of Review to Privy Council refused by Court of Queen's Bench.
Young v. Lambert.	L. R. 3 P. C. 142 ; 6 Moo. N. S. 406 ; 39 L. J. 21 ; 22 L. T. 499 ; 18 W. R. 197.	Judgment reversed.

CASES IN THE QUEBEC COURTS CARRIED TO THE SUPREME COURT OF CANADA.

CASE.	REPORT ON APPEAL.	RESULT OF APPEAL.
Abbott v. Macdonald, 21 L. C. J. 311.	3 S. C. R. 278.	Appeal from Court of Review quashed.
Accident Ins. Co. v. Young (M. L. R. 7 Q. B. 447) 6 S. C. 3.	20 S. C. R. 280.	Judgment reversed.
Ætna Life Ins. Co. v. Brodie (20 L. C. J. 286).	5 S. C. R. 1.	Judgment reversed.
Allen v. Hanson (16 Q. L. R. 79).	18 S. C. R. 667.	Judgment affirmed.
Allen v. Merchants' Marine Ins. Co. (M. L. R. 3 Q. B. 293).	15 S. C. R. 488.	Judgment affirmed.
Anglo-Continental Guano Works Co. v. Emerald Phosphate Co. (M. L. R. 7 Q. B. 196 ; 21 R. L. 288).	21 S. C. R. 422.	Appeal quashed.
Ayotte v. Boucher (3 Dor. Q. B. 123).	9 S. C. R. 460.	Judgment affirmed.
Bain v. City of Montreal (2 Dor. Q. B. 221).	8 S. C. R. 252.	Judgment affirmed.
Banque Jacques Cartier v. Giraldi (26 L. C. J. 110).	9 S. C. R. 597.	Judgment affirmed.
Bank of Toronto v. Perkins (1 Dor. Q. B. 357).	8 S. C. R. 603.	Judgment affirmed.
Baptist v. Baptist (Q. R. 1 Q. B. 447).	21 S. C. R. 425.	Motion to quash appeal refused.
Barnard v. Molson (M. L. R. 3 Q. B. 348) 2 S. C. 143.	15 S. C. R. 716.	Judgment affirmed.
(M. L. R. 6 Q. B. 201) 5 S. C. 374.	18 S. C. R. 622.	Appeal quashed ; judgment not final.
Beaubien v. Bernatchez (14 R. L. 193).	S. C. Dig. 433.	Appeal quashed ; amount not sufficient.
Beausoliel v. Normand (2 Dor. Q. B. 215).	9 S. C. R. 711.	Judgment affirmed.
Bell v. Rickaby (3 Q. L. R. 243).	2 S. C. R. 560.	Judgment reversed.
Bellechasse Election Case [Deslauriers v. Larue] (5 Q. L. R. 191; 6 Q. L. R. 100).	5 S. C. R. 91.	Judgment in 5 Q. L. R. 191 reversed; later judgment affirmed.
Bellemare v. Dansereau (18 R. L. 250).	16 S. C. R. 180.	Judgment reversed.
Benning v. Atlantic & N. W. Ry. Co. (M. L. R. 6 Q. B. 385) 5 S. C. 136.	20 S. C. R. 177.	Judgment affirmed.
Bernier v. Tremblay (Q. R. 1 Q. B. 176) 17 Q. L. R. 185.	21 S. C. R. 409.	Judgment affirmed.
Berthier Election Case [Genereux v. Cuthbert] (6 L. N. 74).	9 S. C. R. 102.	Judgment affirmed.
Bigaouette v. North Shore Ry. Co. (19 R. L. 488).	17 S. C. R. 363.	Judgment reversed.
Black v. Walker (M. L. R. 1 Q. B. 214 ; 8 L. N. 67) 5 L. N. 415.	S. C. Dig. 768.	Judgment affirmed.
Boulanger v. Grand Trunk Ry. Co. (11 Q. L. R. 254).	S. C. Dig. 733.	Judgment affirmed.

CASE.	REPORT ON APPEAL.	RESULT OF APPEAL.
Bourget v. Blanchard (9 Q. L. R. 262).	S. C. Dig. 423.	Leave to appeal refused.
Boyce v. Phœnix Mutual Ins. Co. (M. L. R. 2 Q. B. 323).	14 S. C. R. 723.	Judgment affirmed.
Brady v. Stewart (M. L. R. 2 Q. B. 272).	15 S. C. R. 82.	Judgment affirmed.
Brassard v. Langevin [Charlevoix Election] (2 Q. L. R. 323) (9 R. L.153).	{ 1 S. C. R. 145.	Judgment reversed.
	2 S. C. R. 319.	Appeal from judgment on preliminary objection quashed.
Breakey v. Carter, 7 Q. L. R. 286.	S. C. Dig. 463.	Judgment reversed.
Brown v. Leclere (Q. R. 1 Q. B. 234).	22 S. C. R. 53.	Judgment affirmed.
Brown v. Dominion Salvage & Wrecking Co., 20 R. L. 557.	20 S. C. R. 203.	Appeal quashed; amount not sufficient.
Brunet v. L'Association Pharmaceutique de Quebec (M. L. R. 2 Q. B. 362) 1 S. C. 485.	14 S. C. R. 738.	Judgment affirmed.
Bulmer v. Dufresne (1 L. N. 303) 21 L. C. J. 98.	S. C. Dig. 873.	Judgment affirmed.
Cadwell v. Shaw (M. L. R. 4 Q. B. 246).	17 S. C. R. 357.	Judgment affirmed.
Canada Investment & Agency Co. v. McGregor (Q. R. 1 Q. B. 197) M. L. R. 6 S. C. 196.	21 S. C. R. 499.	Judgment affirmed.
Canada Shipping Co. v. Hudon Cotton Co. (2 Dor. Q. B. 356).	13 S. C. R. 401.	Judgment affirmed.
Canadian Bank of Commerce v. Stevenson (Q. R. 1 Q. B. 371).	——	Judgment reversed.
Carrier v. Bender (12 Q. L. R. 19).	15 S. C. R. 19.	Judgment reversed.
Central Vermont Ry. Co. v. Town of St. Johns (30 L. C. J. 122 ; M. L. R. 4 Q. B. 466).	14 S. C. R. 288 ; aff. by Pr. Coun. 14 App. Cas. 590.	Judgment reversed.
Chalifoux v. Canadian Pacific Ry. Co. (M. L. R. 3 Q. B. 324) 2 S. C. 171.	S. C. Dig. 749.	Judgment reversed.
Chamberlin v. Klock (31 L. C. J. 29).	15 S. C. R. 325.	Judgment affirmed.
Champoux v. Lapierre (3 L. N. 302).	S. C. Dig. 426.	Appeal quashed; amount not sufficient.
Charlebois v. Charlebois [2 cases] (26 L. C. J. 364, 376).	S. C. Dig. 592.	Judgment affirmed.
Cimon v. Perreault [Charlevoix Election] (10 R. L. 651).	5 S. C. R. 133.	Judgment reversed.
Claude v Weir (M. L. R. 4 Q. B. 197) 2 S. C. 326.	16 S. C. R. 575.	Judgment affirmed.
Compagnie de Villas du Cap Gibraltar v. Hughes (3 Dor. Q. B. 175).	11 S. C. R. 537.	Judgment affirmed.
Connolly v. Provincial Ins. Co. (1 L. N. 33) 3 Q. L. R. 6.	5 S. C. R. 258.	Judgment reversed.
Coté v. Stadacona Ins. Co. (6 Q. L. R. 147) 5 Q. L. R. 133.	6 S. C. R. 193.	Judgment reversed.
Cowen v. Evans, 21 R. L. 285.	22 S. C. R. 328.	Appeal quashed; amount not sufficient.
Cross v. Windsor Hotel Co. (M. L. R. 2 Q. B. 8 ; 4 Dor. Q. B. 280).	12 S. C. R. 624.	Judgment affirmed.
Cushing v. Ducondu (3 L. N. 350).	6 S. C. R. 425 *sub nom.* Dupuy v. Ducondu ; rev. by Pr. Coun. 9 App. Cas. 150.	Judgment reversed, but restored on further appeal.

CASE.	REPORT ON APPEAL.	RESULT OF APPEAL.
Danjou v. Marquis, 3 Q. L. R. 335.	3 S. C. R. 251.	Appeal from Superior Ct. in mandamus quashed.
Dansereau v. Letourneux (M. L. R. 1 Q. B. 357 ; 4 Dor. Q. B. 220) 5 L. N. 339.	12 S. C. R. 307.	Judgment affirmed.
Darling v. Barsalou (1 Dor. Q. B. 218).	9 S. C. R. 677.	Judgment reversed.
Darling v. Brown (21 L. C. J. 92).	1 S. C. R. 360.	Judgment affirmed.
Daveluy v. La Société Canadienne Française de Construction (M. L. R. 7 Q. B. 417).	20 S. C. R. 449.	Judgment reversed.
Davidson v. Lord (M. L. R. 1 Q. B. 445).	13 S. C. R. 166.	Judgment affirmed.
Dawson v. McDonald (10 R. L. 640).	S. C. Dig. 586.	Judgment affirmed.
Demers v. Duhaime (14 Q. L. R. 16).	16 S. C. R. 366.	Judgment affirmed.
Desilets v. Gingras (10 R. L. 275).	S. C. Dig. 212.	Judgment reversed.
Dorion v. Crowley (30 L. C. J. 65).	S. C. Dig. 709.	Judgment reversed on ground not taken below.
Dorion v. Dorion (M. L. R. 1 Q. B. 483 ; 4 Dor. Q. B. 213).	13 S. C. R. 193.	Judgment reversed in part.
(18 R. L. 645).	20 S. C. R. 430.	Judgment reversed.
Dubuc v. Kidston, 7 Q. L. R. 43.	S. C. Dig. 779.	Judgment reversed.
Dufresne v. Dixon (32 L. C. J. 80).	16 S. C. R. 596.	Judgment affirmed. ·
Dun v. Cossette (M. L. R. 5 Q. B. 42 ; 33 L. C. J. 94) 3 S. C. 345.	18 S. C. R. 222.	Judgment reversed as to damages.
Dupras v. Lamoureux, 16 R. L. 243.	19 S. C. R. 531 *sub nom.* Brossard v. Dupras.	Judgment reversed.
Dussault v. Belleau [Levis Election Case] (10 Q. L. R. 247).	11 S. C. R. 133.	Judgment affirmed.
Exchange Bank v. Fletcher (M. L. R. 7 Q. B. 11 ; 19 R. L. 377 ; 34 L. C. J. 130).	19 S. C. R. 278.	Judgment affirmed
Exchange Bank v. La Banque du Peuple (M. L. R. 3 Q. B. 232) 1 S. C. 231.	S. C. Dig. 79.	Judgment affirmed by equal division.
Fairbanks v. Barlow (M. L. R. 2 Q. B. 332).	14 S. C. R. 217.	Judgment affirmed.
Farwell v. Ontario Car Co. (M. L. R. 6 Q. B. 91) 3 S. C. 228. Farwell v. Wallbridge (M. L. R. 6 Q. B. 77).	18 S. C. R. 1.	Judgment in both cases affirmed.
Fauteaux v. Montreal Loan & Mortgage Co. (22 L. C. J. 282).	3 S. C. R. 411.	Judgment affirmed.
Fisk v. Stevens (3 Dor. Q. B. 293 ; 6 L. N. 329) 5 L. N. 79.	S. C. Dig. 235; 8 L. N. 42.	Judgment reversed.
Fraser v. Jones (12 Q. L. R. 333).	13 S. C. R. 342.	Judgment varied.
Fraser v. Pouliot, 3 Q. L. R. 349.	4 S. C. R. 515.	Judgment affirmed.
Gilman v. Exchange Bank of Canada (16 R. L. 663).	17 S. C. R. 108.	Judgment reversed.
Gilman v. Gilbert (M. L. R. 3 Q. B. 402 ; 32 L. C. J. 138).	16 S. C. R. 189.	Appeal quashed.
Grange v. McLennan (3 Dor. Q. B. 212).	9 S. C. R. 385.	Judgment affirmed.
Grant v. Beaudry (2 Dor. Q. B. 197 ; 4 L. N. 393) 2 L. N. 354.	S. C. Dig. 581.	· Appeal affirmed.

CASE.	REPORT ON APPEAL.	RESULT OF APPEAL.
Great North Western Telegraph Co. v. Montreal Telegraph Co. (M. L. R. 6 Q. B. 257) 6 S. C. 74; 34 L. C. J. 35.	20 S. C. R. 170.	Judgment affirmed.
Gregoire v. Gregoire (M. L. R. 2 Q. B. 228; 4 Dor. Q. B. 308; 30 L. C. J. 286; 12 Q. L. R. 32).	13 S. C. R. 319.	Judgment affirmed.
Hagar v. Seath (M. L. R. 6 Q. B. 394) 5 S. C. 426.	18 S. C. R. 715.	Appeal quashed.
Hall v. Mayor of Montreal (6 L. N. 155; 27 L. C. J. 129).	12 S. C. R. 74.	Judgment affirmed.
Hampson v. Vineberg, (33 L. C. J. 185); M. L. R. 3 S. C. 434.	19 S. C. R. 369.	Appeal quashed.
Hannan v. Ross (M. L. R. 6 Q. B. 222). 2 S. C. 395.	19 S. C. R. 227.	Judgment affirmed.
Hardy v. Filiatrault (17 R. L. 27).	17 S. C. R. 292.	Judgment reversed.
Harrington v. Corse (26 L. C. J. 79).	9 S. C. R. 412.	Judgment reversed.
Hart v. Joyce (8 R. L. 209).	1 S. C. R. 321.	Judgment affirmed.
Hathaway v. Chaplin (M. L. R. 7 Q. B. 317).	21 S. C. R. 23.	Judgment affirmed.
Heffernan v. Walsh (M. L. R. 2 Q. B. 482; 33 L. C. J. 46).	14 S. C. R. 738.	Appeal quashed.
Holland v. Mitchell, 15 R. L. 214.	16 S. C. R. 687.	Judgment affirmed.
Johnston v. Ministers, etc., St. Andrew's Church, 18 L. C. J. 113; 5 R. L. 487.	1 S. C. R. 235.	Judgment reversed.
Kane v. Wright (1 Dor. Q. B. 297; 4 L. N. 15) 1 L. N. 482.	S. C. Dig. 596.	Judgment affirmed.
Kerr v. Davis (M. L. R. 5 Q. B. 156).	17 S. C. R. 235.	Judgment reversed in part.
Labelle v. Barbeau (33 L. C. J. 252).	16 S. C. R. 390.	Appeal quashed; amount not sufficient.
Labelle v. City of Montreal (M. L. R. 7 Q. B. 468) 2 S. C. 56.	14 S. C. R. 741.	Judgment reversed.
Lamarche v. L'Heureux (11 Q. L. R. 342) 13 Q. L. R. 129.	12 S. C. R. 460.	Judgment reversed.
Langevin v. Les Commissioners d'Ecole de St. Marc. (M. L. R. 7 Q. B. 390; 19 R. L. 301).	18 S. C. R. 599.	Appeal from interlocutory judgment in *mandamus* quashed.
Langlois v. Valin [Montmorency Election] (5 Q. L. R. 1).	3 S. C. R. 1.	Judgment affirmed.
Lapierre v. L'Union St. Joseph de Montreal (21 L. C. J. 332).	4 S. C. R. 164.	Judgment reversed.
Lapierre v. Rodier (Q. R. 1 Q. B. 515).	21 S. C. R. 69.	Appeal quashed; amount not sufficient.
Larin v. Chapman (1 L. N. 458).	4 S. C. R. 349.	Judgment affirmed.
Larue v. Kinghorn (Q. R. 2 Q. B. 263).	22 S. C. R. 347.	Appeal quashed; amount not sufficient.
Larue v. Rattray (12 Q. L. R. 258).	15 S. C. R. 102.	Judgment reversed.
Lasnier v. Collette, 5 L. N. 412.	13 S. C. R. 563.	Judgment varied.
Lasalle v. Bergeron (1 Dor. Q. B. 257).	S. C. Dig. 495.	Judgment affirmed.
Lefebvre v. Monette (32 L. C. J. 195).	16 S. C. R. 387.	Appeal quashed; amount not sufficient.
Lefeuntun v. Verouneau (Q. R. 1 Q. B. 277).	22 S. C. R. 203.	Judgment reversed.

CASE.	REPORT ON APPEAL.	RESULT OF APPEAL.
Leger v. Fournier (M. L. R. 3 Q. B. 124) 1 S. C. 360.	14 S C. R. 314.	Judgment affirmed.
Lionais v. Molsons Bank (26 L. C. J. 271).	10 S. C. R. 526.	Judgment reversed.
Longueuil Navigation Co. v. City of Montreal (M. L. R. 3 Q. B. 172) 2 S. C. 18.	15 S. C. R. 566.	Judgment reversed.
Loranger, Atty.-Gen. v. Reed (3 Dor. Q. B. 33 ; 26 L. C. J. 331).	8 S. C. R. 408 *sub nom.* Reed v. Mousseau ; aff. by Pr. Coun. 10 App. Cas. 141.	Judgment reversed.
Low v. Gemley (M. L. R. 5 Q. B. 186) 4 S. C. 92.	18 S. C. R. 685.	Judgment affirmed.
Mackinnon v. Kerouack (15 R. L. 34).	15 S. C. R. 111.	Judgment affirmed.
Magnan v. Dugas [Montcalm Election] (12 R. L. 226).	9 S. C. R. 93.	Judgment affirmed.
Magog Textile & Print Co. v. Price (12 Q. L. R. 200). Magog Textile & Print Co. v. Dobell (12 Q. L. R. 204).	14 S. C. R. 664.	Judgment affirmed.
Mail Printing Co. v. Laflamme (M. L. R. 4 Q. B. 84) 2 S. C. 146 ; 30 L. C. J. 87.	S. C. Dig. 493.	Judgment varied.
Martindale v. Powers (Q. R. 1 Q. B. 144).	Not yet reported.	Judgment affirmed.
Miller v. Coleman (2 Dor. Q. B. 33 ; 25 L. C. J. 196).	S. C. Dig. 301.	Judgment reversed.
Mitchell v. Mitchell (M. L. R. 4 Q. B. 191) 3 S. C. 31 ; 31 L. C. J. 178.	16 S. C. R. 722.	Judgment affirmed.
Mitchell v. Trenholme (Q. R. 2 Q. B. 164).	22 S. C. R. 331.	Appeal quashed.
Moffatt v. Burland (4 Dor. Q. B. 59 ; 28 L. C. J. 214).	11 S. C. R. 76.	Judgment reversed.*
Moir v. Village of Huntingdon (M. L. R. 7 Q. B. 281).	19 S. C. R. 363.	Appeal for costs only not entertained.
Molson v. Lambe (31 L. C. J. 59 : M. L. R. 2 Q. B. 381) 1 S. C. 264.	15 S. C. R. 253.	Judgment affirmed.
Montreal, City of, v. Les Ecclesiastiques, etc., de St. Sulpice (32 L. C. J. 13 ; M. L. R. 4 Q. B. 1) 2 S. C. 265 ; 1 S. C. 450.	16 S. C. R. 399.	Judgment reversed ; leave to appeal to Pr. Coun. refused.
Montreal City Passenger Ry. Co. v. Parker (7 L. N. 194).	S. C. Dig. 731.	Judgment reversed.
Montreal Street Ry. Co. v. Ritchie (M. L. R. 5 Q. B. 77) 3 S. C. 232.	16 S. C. R. 622.	Judgment affirmed.
Moodie v. Jones (M. L. R. 6 Q. B. 354).	19 S. C. R. 266.	Judgment affirmed
Moreau v. Price (15 Q. L. R. 241).	18 S. C. R. 303 *sub nom.* Price v. Mercier.	Judgment reversed.
Morgan v. Coté (3 L. N. 274).	7 S. C. R. 1.	Judgment reversed.
Morris v. Connecticut & Passumpsic Rivers Ry. Co. (M. L. R. 2 Q. B. 303).	14 S. C. R. 318.	Judgment affirmed.
Morrison v. McCuaig, 4 L. N. 151.	S. C. Dig. 642.	Judgment affirmed.
Morse v. Martin (28 L. C. J. 236) 5 L. N. 99.	S. C. Dig. 839.	Judgment affirmed.
Munn v. Berger (27 L. C. J. 349 ; 6 L. N. 363).	10 S. C. R. 512.	Judgment reversed.
McArthur v. Brown (13 Q. L. R. 168).	17 S. C. R. 61.	Judgment affirmed.
McBain v. Blachford (M. L. R. 6 Q. B. 273).	19 S. C. R. 42. 20 S. C. R. 269.	Motion to quash appeal refused. Judgment affirmed.

* But see Porteous v. Reynar, 13 App. Cas. 120.

CASE.	REPORT ON APPEAL.	RESULT OF APPEAL.
McCaffrey v. Ball, 34 L. C. J. 91.	20 S. C. R. 319.	Judgment reversed.
McCorkill v. Knight (1 L. N. 42).	3 S. C. R. 233.	Judgment affirmed.
McFarlane v. St. Cesaire (M. L. R. 2 Q. B. 160).	14 S. C. R. 738.	Judgment affirmed.
McGreevy v. Boomer (9 R. L. 587).	S. C. Dig. 139.	Judgment affirmed.
McGreevy v. Leduc (10 Q. L. R. 188).	S. C. Dig. 801.	Judgment reversed.
McGreevy v. McCarron (12 Q. R. L. 373; 14 R. L. 422).	13 S. C. R. 378.	Judgment affirmed.
McLachlan v. Accident Ins. Co. (34 L. C.J. 43 ; M. L. R. 6 Q. B. 39) 4 S. C. 365.	18 S. C. R. 627.	Appeal quashed ; judgment not final.
McManamy v. City of Sherbrooke (M. L. R. 6 Q. B. 409 ; 19 R. L. 423).	18 S. C. R. 594.	Appeal quashed ; amount not sufficient.
McMillan v. Hedge (M. L. R. 1 Q. B. 376; 4 Dor. Q. B. 269).	14 S. C. R. 736.	Judgment affirmed.
Nordheimer v. Alexander (33 L. C. J. 175; M. L. R. 6 Q. B. 402) 3 S. C. 283.	19 S. C. R. 248.	Judgment affirmed.
North Shore Ry. Co. v. Beaudet (11 Q. L. R. 239).	15 S. C. R. 44.	Judgment reversed.
North Shore Ry. Co. v. McWillie (M. L. R. 5 Q. B. 122 ; 34 L. C. J. 55).	17 S. C. R. 511.	Judgment affirmed.
North Shore Ry. Co. v. Pion (4 Dor. Q. B. 258; 12 Q. L. R. 205).	14 S. C. R. 677; aff. by Pr. Coun., 14 App. Cas. 612.	Judgment reversed.
O'Brien v. Caron [Quebec County Election] (15 R. L. 697).	14 S. C. R. 429, 434.	Appeal quashed.
Ontario Bank v. Chaplin (M. L. R. 5 Q. B. 407) 15 R. L. 435.	20 S. C. R. 152.	Judgment affirmed.
Ontario & Quebec Ry. Co. v. Marcheterre, 17 R. L. 409.	17 S. C. R. 141.	Appeal quashed ; judgment not final.
Ottawa, County of, v. Montreal, etc., Ry. Co. (M. L. R. 1 Q. B. 46 ; 28 L. C. J. 29) 26 L. C. J. 148 ; 5 L. N. 132.	14 S. C. R. 193.	Judgment affirmed.
Owens v. Bedell (M. L. R. 7 Q. B. 395).	19 S. C. R. 137.	Judgment affirmed.
Petry v. La Caisse d'Economie de Notre Dame, 16 Q. L. R. 193.	19 S. C. R. 713.	Judgment affirmed.
Pigeon v. Recorder's Court (M. L. R. 6 Q. B. 60 ; 33 L. C. J. 221).	17 S. C. R. 495.	Judgment affirmed.
Pinsonneault v. Hebert (7 L. N. 276).	13 S. C. R. 450.	Judgment reversed.
Poulin v. Corporation of Quebec (2 Dor. Q. B. 103 ; 7 Q. L. R. 337).	9 S. C. R. 185.	Judgment affirmed.
Prefontaine v. Dufresne } Prefontaine v. Vallee. } (Q. R. 1 Q. B. 330)	21 S. C. R. 607.	Judgment affirmed.
Prince v. Gagnon (2 Dor. Q. B. 74).	7 S. C. R. 386.	Judgment reversed.
Quebec, City of, v. Quebec Gas Co. (17 Q. L. R. 150).	20 S. C. R. 230.	Appeal in case attacking a by-law quashed.
Quebec, City of, v. Quebec Street Ry. Co. (13 Q. L. R. 205 ; 12 Q. L. R. 317).	15 S. C. R. 164.	Judgment reversed.
Quebec Harbor Commissioners v. Peters (16 Q. L. R. 129) 15 Q. L. R. 277.	19 S. C. R. 685.	Judgment reversed.
Quebec, Montmorenci & Charlevoix Ry. Co. v. Mathieu, 15 Q. L. R. 300.	19 S. C. R. 426.	Judgment affirmed.
Quebec Warehouse Co. v. Town of Levis (3 Dor. Q. B. 322) 9 Q. L. R. 305.	11 S. C. R. 666.	Judgment reversed.

CASE.	REPORT ON APPEAL.	RESULT OF APPEAL.
Raphael v. McFarlane (M. L. R. 5 Q. B. 273).	18 S. C. R. 183.	Judgment reversed.
Reeves v. Geriken (2 L. N. 67).	10 S. C. R. 616 *sub nom.* Reeves v. Perreault.	Judgment reversed.
Reg. v. Abrahams (1 Dor. Q. B. 126; 24 L. C. J. 325).	6 S. C. R. 10.	Judgment reversed.
Reg. v. Downie (M. L. R. 3 Q. B. 360).	15 S. C. R. 358.	Judgment affirmed.
Reg. v. Morin (16 Q. L. R. 366).	18 S. C. R. 407.	Judgment affirmed.
Reg. v. Scott (21 L. C. J. 225).	2 S. C. R. 349.	Judgment reversed.
Robinson v. Canadian Pacific Ry. Co. (M. L. R. 2 Q. B. 25).	14 S. C. R. 105.	Judgment reversed.
(M. L. R. 6 Q. B. 118) 5 S. C. 225; 33 L. C. J. 145.	19 S. C. R. 292; rev. by Pr. Coun. [1892] A. C. 481.	Judgment reversed, but restored on further appeal.
Ross v. Holland (M. L. R. 2 Q. B. 316).	19 S. C. R. 566.	Judgment reversed.
Ross v. Ross (7 L. N. 65) 5 L. N. 197. (Q. R. 2 Q. B. 413) 16 L. N. 92.	S. C. Dig. 306.	Judgment affirmed. Judgment partly reversed.
Royal Institution of Learning v. Scottish Union Ins. Co. (M. L. R. 6 Q. B. 458).	18 S. C. R. 615 *sub nom.* Barrington v. Scot. Union.	Appeal quashed; judgment not final.
Russell v. Lafrançois (2 Dor. Q. B. 245).	8 S. C. R. 335; leave to appeal to Pr. Coun. refused.	Judgment reversed.
Sangster v. Hood (M. L. R. 5 Q. B. 384; 18 R. L. 40).	16 S. C. R. 723.	Appeal quashed; amount not sufficient.
School Commissioners of Ste. Victoire v. Hus (M. L. R. 7 Q. B. 330).	19 S. C. R. 477.	Judgment affirmed.
Schwersenski v. Vineberg (M. L. R. 7 Q. B. 137).	19 S. C. R. 243.	Judgment affirmed.
Shaw v. McKenzie (25 L. C. J. 40) 23 L. C. J. 52; 2 L. N. 5.	6 S. C. R. 181.	Judgment reversed.
Sheridan v. Ottawa Agricultural Ins. Co. (2 L. N. 206).	5 S. C. R. 157.	Judgment affirmed.
Skelton v. Evans (M. L. R. 3 Q. B. 325; 31 L. C. J. 307)	16 S. C. R. 637.	Judgment affirmed.
Soulanges Election Case [Cholette v. Bain] (7 L. N. 220).	10 S. C. R. 652.	Judgment reversed.
Stephens v. Chaussé (M. L. R. 3 Q. B. 270).	15 S. C. R. 379.	Judgment affirmed.
Stephens v. Gillespie (M. L. R. 3 Q. B. 167).	14 S. C. R. 709.	Judgment affirmed.
Ste. Anne, Corporation of, v. Reburn (M. L. R. 1 Q. B. 200; 4 Dor. Q. B. 192).	15 S. C. R. 92.	Judgment affirmed.
St. James v. Corporation of St. Gabriel (12 R. L. 15).	S. C. Dig. 147.	Judgment affirmed.
St. Louis v. Senecal (M. L. R. 5 Q. B. 332; 33 L. C. J. 325).	18 S. C. R. 587 *sub nom.* St. Louis v. Dansereau.	Judgment affirmed.
St. Louis v. Shaw (2 Dor. Q. B. 374).	8 S. C. R. 385.	Judgment affirmed.
Sweeny v. Bank of Montreal, 5 L. N. 66.	12 S. C. R. 661; aff. by Pr. Coun. 12 App. Cas. 617.	Judgment reversed.
Thibaudeau v. Benning (17 R. L. 173; 33 L. C. J. 39; M. L. R. 5 Q. B. 425) 2 S. C. 338.	20 S. C. R. 110 *sub nom.* Simpson v. Thibaudeau.	Judgment affirmed.
Thompson v. Molson's Bank, 8 L. N. 363.	16 S. C. R. 664.	Judgment affirmed.

CASE.	REPORT ON APPEAL.	RESULT OF APPEAL.
Three Rivers, Corporation of, v. Major (2 Dor. Q. B. 84; 8 Q. L. R. 181; 11 R. L. 238).	S. C. Dig. 422.	Appeal quashed ; case not originating in Superior Court.
Three Rivers, Corporation of, v. Sulte (5 L. N. 331).	11 S. C. R. 25.	Judgment affirmed.
Treacey v. Ligget (3 Dor. Q. B. 247).	9 S. C. R. 441.	Judgment reversed.
Vercheres, Corporation of, v. Village of Varennes (M. L. R. 7 Q. B. 368) 7 S. C. 3.	19 S. C. R. 365.	Appeal in action attacking by-law quashed.
Vezina v. New York Life Ins. Co. (3 L. N. 322 ; 25 L. C. J. 232).	6 S. C. R. 30.	Judgment reversed.
Vezina v. Quebec North Shore Turnpike Road Trustees (3 Dor. Q. B. 65).	S. C. Dig. 758.	Judgment affirmed.
Wadsworth v. McCord (M. L. R. 2 Q. B. 113 ; 11 Q. L. R. 232).	12 S. C. R. 466 ; aff. by Pr. Coun. 14 App. Cas. 631.	Judgment reversed.
Western Assur. Co. v. Scanlan (15 R. L. 449).	13 S. C. R. 207.	Judgment reversed.
Wheeler v. Black (M. L. R. 2 Q. B. 139).	14 S. C. R. 242.	Judgment affirmed.
Wilson v. Grand Trunk Ry. Co. (2 Dor. Q. B. 131).	S. C. Dig. 722.	Judgment affirmed.
Wilson v. Lacoste (M. L. R. 6 Q. B. 316).	20 S. C. R. 218.	Judgment affirmed.
Wylie v. City of Montreal (M. L. R. 1 Q. B. 367 ; 4 Dor. Q. B. 245) 7 L. N. 26.	12 S. C. R. 384.	Judgment reversed.
Yon v. Cassidy (33 L. C. J. 106).	18 S. C. R. 713.	Judgment affirmed.
Young v. Rattray (12 Q. L. R. 168 ; 8 L. N. 10).	S. C. Dig. 149.	Judgment reversed.

[57]

CASES IN THE COURTS OF NOVA SCOTIA CARRIED TO THE PRIVY COUNCIL.

CASE.	REPORT ON APPEAL.	RESULT OF APPEAL.
American, The (Stewart V. A. Rep. 286).	Stewart V. A. Rep. 292n.	Judgment reversed.*
Bank of British North America v. Strong.	1 App. Cas. 307 ; 34 L. T. 627.	Judgment reversed.
Cape Breton, in re.	5 Moo. P. C. 259.	Petition against annexation refused.
Chase, The (Young V. A. Rep. 113).	Young V. A. Rep. 125.	Judgment affirmed.
Cobequid Marine Ins. Co. v. Barteaux	L. R. 6 P. C. 319 ; 32 L. T. 510 ; 23 W. R. 892.	Judgment reversed.
Colonial Bank v. Exchange Bank of Yarmouth (5 R. & G. 125).	11 App. Cas. 84 ; (55 L. J. 14 sub nom. Col. Bank v. Bank of Nova Scotia) 54 L. T. 256 ; 34 W. R. 417.	Judgment reversed.
Cossman v. British American Assur. Co. (6 R. & G. 457). Cossman v. West (16 R. & G. 461).	13 App. Cas. 160 ; 57 L. J. 17 ; 58 L. T. 122 ; 4 Times L. R. 65.	Judgment reversed.
Des Barres v. Shey (2 N. S. D. 327).	29 L. T. 592 ; 22 W. R. 273.	Judgment affirmed.
Exchange Bank v. Blethen (5 R. & G. 533).	10 App. Cas. 293 ; 53 L. T. 537 ; 33 W.R. 801.	Judgment affirmed.
Fly, The (Stewart V. A. Rep. 171).	Stewart V. A. Rep. 173n.	Judgment affirmed.*
Furieuse, La (Stewart V. A. Rep. 177).	Stewart V. A. Rep. 185n.	Judgment affirmed.*
Geldert v. Municipality of Pictou (23 N. S. Rep. 483.	[1893] A.C. 524; 9 Times L. R. 638.	Judgment reversed.
Happy Couple, The (Stewart V. A. Rep. 65).	Stewart V. A. Rep. 76n.	Judgment affirmed.
Hill v. Goodall.	3 Murd. Epit. 145.	Judgment reversed.
Mott v. Lockhart.	8 App. Cas. 568 ; 52 L. J. 61.	Judgment reversed.
McLean v. McKay.	L. R. 5 P. C. 327; 29 L. T. 352; 21 W. R. 798.	Judgment reversed.
McLeod v. McNab.	[1891] A. C. 471 ; 60 L. J. 70 ; 65 L. T. 266.	Judgment affirmed.

* By High Court of Admiralty.

CASE.	REPORT ON APPEAL.	RESULT OF APPEAL.
McSweeney v. Wallace (2 Old. 332).	L. R. 2 P. C. 180 ; 5 Moo. N. S. 244 ; 37 L. J. 39 ; 16 W. R. 1088.	Judgment reversed.
Nancy, The (Stewart V. A. Rep. 28).	Stewart V. A. Rep. 38n.	Judgment reversed.*
Parker v. Kenny (5 R. & G. 457).	Wheeler P.C. Law, 293; 6 Can Gaz. 174.	Judgment affirmed.
Robertson v. Grant.	Wheeler P. C. Law, 14.	Judgment affirmed.
Snow v. Morton (2 N. S. D. 237).	29 L. T. 591.	Judgment reversed.
Taylor v. Archibald (3 N. S. D. 233).	Wheler P. C. Law 48.	New trial ordered.
Thomas Allen, The, v. Gow.	12 App. Cas. 118 ; 56 L. T. 285.	Judgment varied.
Three Brothers, The (Stewart V. A. Rep. 99).	Stewart V. A. Rep. 100n.	Judgment affirmed.*
United States, The (Stewart V. A. Rep. 116).	Stewart V. A. Rep. 122n.	Judgment reversed.*
Venus, The (Stewart V. A. Rep. 96).	Stewart V. A. Rep. 97.	Judgment affirmed.*
Wallace, in re (1 Old. 654).	L. R. 1 P. C. 283 ; 4 Moo. N. S. 140 ; 36 L. J. 9 ; 15 W. R. 533.	Judgment reversed.
Windsor & Annapolis Ry. Co. v. Western Counties Ry. Co. (R. E. D. 383) 2 R. & G. 280.	7 App Cas. 178 ; 51 L. J. 43 ; 46 L. T. 351.	Judgment affirmed.

* By High Court of Admiralty.

CASES IN THE NOVA SCOTIA COURTS CARRIED TO THE SUPREME COURT OF CANADA.

CASE.	REPORT ON APPEAL.	RESULT OF APPEAL.
Almon v. Providence Washington Ins. Co. (4 R. & G. 533).	S. C. Dig. 390.	Judgment reversed.
Annand v. Tupper (21 N. S. Rep. 11).	16 S. C. R. 718.	Judgment affirmed.
Atty.-Gen. of Canada v. Flint (3 R. & G. 453).	16 S. C. R. 707.	Judgment reversed.
Atty.-Gen. of Nova Scotia v. Axford (5 R. & G. 107) Russ. Eq. D. 429.	13 S. C. R. 294.	Judgment reversed.
Bailey v. Ocean Mutual Marine Ins. Co. (22 N. S. Rep. 5).	19 S. C. R. 153.	Judgment affirmed.
Bank of Liverpool, in re (6 R. & G. 531)	14 S. C. R. 650 sub nom. Mott v. Bank of Nova Scotia.	Judgment reversed.
(22 N. S. Rep. 97).	17 S. C. R. 707 sub nom. Forsythe v. Bank of Nova Scotia.	Judgment affirmed.
Bank of Nova Scotia v. Smith (4 R. & G. 146).	8 S. C. R. 558.	Judgment reversed.
Beamish v. Kaulbach (3 R. & C. 427).	3 S. C. R. 704.	Appeal from Court of Probate quashed.
Boak v. Merchants' Marine Ins. Co. (1 R. & C. 288).	1 S. C. R. 110.	Appeal from order for new trial quashed.
Bowmanville Machine Co. v. Dempster (2 R. & C. 273).	2 S. C. R. 21.	Judgment affirmed.
Bradley v. McLean (2 R. & C. 584).	2 S. C. R. 535.	Judgment reversed.
Brown v. Brookfield (24 N. S. Rep. 476).	22 S. C. R. 398.	Judgment affirmed on different grounds.
Bunker's Island, in re (3 R. & C. 367).	3 S. C. R. 203 sub nom. Wilkins v. Geddes.	Judgment affirmed.
Burnham v. Davison (5 R. & G. 388).	S. C. Dig. 846.	Judgment affirmed.
Butler v. Merchants' Marine Ins. Co. (5 R. & G. 301).	S. C. Dig. 390.	Judgment affirmed.
Caldwell v. Stadacona Ins. Co. (3 R. & G. 218).	11 S. C. R. 212.	Judgment reversed.
Chesley v. Murdoch (2 R. & C. 321).	2 S. C. R. 48.	Judgment affirmed.
Church Wardens of Parrsboro' v. King (2 R. & C. 383).	2 S. C. R. 143 sub nom. Rector, etc., of St. George's Parish v. King.	Judgment reversed.
Clark v. Clark (21 N. S. Rep. 378).	17 S. C. R. 376.	Judgment reversed.
Cogswell v. Holland (21 N. S. Rep. 279) 21 N. S. Rep 155.	17 S. C. R. 420 sub nom. Cogswell v. O'Brien.	Judgment affirmed.
Corbett v. Anchor Marine Ins. Co. (2 R. & G. 375.	9 S. C. R. 73.	Judgment affirmed.
Corbett v. Providence Washington Ins. Co. 3 R. & G. 109).	9 S. C. R. 256.	Judgment reversed.

CASE.	REPORT ON APPEAL.	RESULT OF APPEAL.
Cox v. Gunn (2 R. & C. 528).	3 S. C. R. 296.	Judgment reversed.
Creighton v. Chittick (2 R. & G. 90).	7 S. C. R. 348.	Judgment affirmed.
Cummings v. Gladwin (4 R. & G. 168).	S. C. Dig. 426.	Judgment affirmed.
Cunningham v. Collins (23 N. S. Rep. 350).	21 S. C. R. 139.	Judgment reversed in part.
Dickie v. Woodworth [King's County Election] (4 R. & G. 105).	8 S. C. R. 192.	Appeal quashed.
(19 N. S. Rep. 96).	14 S. C. R. 734.	Judgment affirmed.
Doull v. Western Assur. Co. (6 R. & G. 478).	12 S. C. R. 446.	Judgment reversed.
Duggan v. Duggan (22 N. S. Rep. 20).	17 S. C. R. 343.	Judgment reversed.
Eisenhauer v. Nova Scotia Marine Ins. Co. (24 N. S. Rep. 205).	None.	Judgment affirmed.
Ells v. Black (19 N. S. Rep. 222).	14 S. C. R. 740.	Judgment affirmed.
Esson v. Wood (4 R. & G. 276).	9 S. C. R. 239.	Judgment reversed.
Fairbanks v. Kuhn (2 R. & G. 147).	S. C. Dig. 845 *sub nom.* Creighton v. Kuhn.	Judgment affirmed.
Fielding v. Mott (6 R. & G. 339).	14 S. C. R. 254.	Judgment affirmed,
Fisher v. Anderson (1 R. & G. 177).	4 S. C. R. 406.	Judgment reversed.
Fitzrandolph v. Mutual Relief Soc. (21 N. S. Rep. 274).	17 S. C. R. 333.	Judgment affirmed.
Foot v. Foot (20 N. S. Rep. 71).	15 S. C. R. 699.	Judgment affirmed.
Fraser v. Wallace (2 R. & C. 337).	2 S. C. R. 522.	Judgment affirmed.
Fraser, Simon, *in re* (1 R. & G. 354).	S. C. Dig. 421 *sub nom.* Fraser v. Tupper.	Appeal in *habeas corpus* case not entertained.
Fuller v. Pearson (23 N. S. Rep. 263).	21 S. C. R. 337 *sub nom.* Chandler Electric Co. v. Fuller.	Judgment affirmed.
Gallagher v. Taylor (1 R. & G. 279).	5 S. C. R. 368.	Judgment reversed.
Gates v. Davidson (5 R. & G. 431).	S. C. Dig. 847. _	Judgment affirmed.
Grant v. Cameron (23 N. S. Rep. 50).	18 S. C. R. 716.	Judgment affirmed.
Gregory v. Halifax & Cape Breton Coal & Ry. Co. (4 R. & G. 436).	S. C. Dig. 727.	Judgment affirmed.
Guildford v. Anglo-French. S. S. Co. (2 R. & G. 54).	9 S. C. R. 303.	Judgment affirmed.
Halifax Banking Co. v. Creighton (22 N. S. Rep. 321).	18 S. C. R. 140.	Judgment reversed.
Hannon v. McLean (3 R. & C. 101).	3 S. C. R. 706.	Judgment reversed.
Hart v. Troop (2 R. & G. 351).	7 S. C. R. 512.	Judgment affirmed.
Harvey v. Pictou Bank (19 N. S. Rep. 196).	14 S. C. R. 617.	Judgment affirmed.
Hospital for insane, *in re* (2 R. & C. 501).	3 S. C. R. 332 *sub nom.* Kearney v. Kean.	Judgment reversed.
Howard v. Lancashire Ins. Co. (5 R. & G. 172).	11 S. C. R. 92.	Judgment affirmed.

CASE.	REPORT ON APPEAL.	RESULT OF APPEAL.
Hubley v. Archibald (22 N. S. Rep. 27).	18 S. C. R. 116.	Judgment reversed.
International Coal Co. v. County of Cape Breton (24 N. S. Rep. 496).	22 S. C. R. 305.	Judgment reversed.
Johnson, G. R., *in re* (7 R. & G. 51).	S. C. Dig. 329.	Judgment in *habeas corpus* case affirmed.
Jones v. Johns (20 N. S. Rep. 378).	15 S. C. R. 398 *sub nom.* Shorey v. Jones.	Judgment affirmed.
Joyce v. Halifax Street Ry. Co. (21 N. S. Rep. 531).	17 S. C. R. 709.	Appeal from order for new trial quashed.
(24 N. S. Rep. 113).	22 S. C. R. 258.	Judgment affirmed.
Kearney v. Creelman (6 R. & G. 92).	14 S. C. R. 33.	Judgment affirmed.
Kearney v. Dickson (6 R. & G. 65).	S. C. Dig. 431.	Judgment affirmed.
(20 N. S. Rep. 95).	14 S. C. R. 743.	Judgment reversed.
Kearney v. Oakes (20 N. S. Reps. 30).	18 S. C. R. 148.	Judgment reversed.
Keith v. Anchor Marine Ins. Co. (3 R. C. 402).	9 S. C. R. 483.	Judgment affirmed.
Kenney v. Chisholm (7 R. & G. 497).	S. C. Dig. 539.	Judgment affirmed.
Kenny v. City of Halifax (1 R. & G. 39).	3 S. C. R. 497.	Judgment affirmed.
King v. Seeton (21 N. S. Rep. 20).	18 S. C. R. 712.	Judgment affirmed.
Kinney v. Jones (5 R. & G. 244).	11 S. C. R. 708.	Judgment affirmed.
Lane v. McDonald (2 R. & G. 37).	7 S. C. R. 462.	Judgment affirmed.
Law v. British American Assur. Co. (23 N. S. Rep. 537).	21 S. C. R. 325.	Judgment affirmed.
Lawrence v. Anderson (21 N. S. Rep. 466).	17 S. C. R. 349.	Judgment reversed.
Lecain v. Hosterman (2 R. & C. 229).	S. C. Dig. 827.	Judgment affirmed.
Logan v. Commercial Union Ins. Co. (6 R. & G. 309).	13 S. C. R. 270.	Judgment affirmed.
Lordly v. City of Halifax (24 N. S. Rep. 1).	20 S. C. R. 505.	Judgment reversed.
Merchant's Bank of Halifax v. Whidden (22 N. S. Rep. 200).	19 S. C. R. 53.	Judgment affirmed.
Miller v. Duggan (22 N. S. Rep. 140).	21 S. C. R. 33.	Judgment affirmed.
Moir v. Sovereign Ins. Co. (6 R. & G. 502).	14 S. C. R. 612.	Judgment reversed.
Mooney v. McIntosh (19 N. S. Rep. 419).	14 S. C. R. 740.	Judgment affirmed.
Morrison v. Kandick (2 R. & C. 148).	2 S. C. R. 12.	Appeal from judgment setting aside demurrer quashed.
Moss v. Eureka Woollen Mills Co. (6 R. & G. 274).	11 S. C. R. 91.	Judgment affirmed.
McAllister v. Forsyth (5 R. & G. 151).	12 S. C. R. 1.	Judgment affirmed.
McDonald v. Doull (3 R. & C. 276).	S. C. Dig. 384.	Judgment reversed.
McDonald v. McMaster (5 R. & G. 438).	S. C. Dig. 246.	Judgment reversed.
McIlreith v. Doull (19 N. S. Rep. 311).	14 S. C. R. 739.	Judgment reversed.

CASE.	REPORT ON APPEAL.	RESULT OF APPEAL.
McKay v. Municipality of Cape Breton (21 N. S. Rep. 492).	18 S. C. R. 639.	Judgment affirmed by equal division.
McKenzie v. Corbett (4 R. & G. 50).	S. C. Dig. 384.	Judgment reversed.
McPherson v. McDonald (6 R. & G. 242).	12 S. C. R. 416.	Judgment affirmed.
North American Life Assur. Co. v. Craigen (6 R. & G. 440).	13 S. C. R. 278.	Judgment affirmed.
Nova Scotia Central Ry. Co. v. Halifax Banking Co. (23 N. S. Rep. 172).	21 S. C. R. 536.	Judgment affirmed.
Oakes v. City of Halifax (1 R. & G. 98).	4 S. C. R. 640.	Judgment reversed.
O'Connor v. Merchant's Marine Ins. Co. (20 N. S. Rep. 514).	16 S. C. R. 331.	Judgment affirmed.
O'Connor v. Nova Scotia Telephone Co. (23 N. S. Rep. 509).	22 S. C. R. 276.	Judgment reversed.
O'Donnell v. Confederation Life Assoc. (2 R. & C. 570).	S. C. Dig. 370.	Judgment reversed.
(2 R. & G. 231).	10 S. C. R. 92.	Judgment reversed.
(21 N. S. Rep. 169).	16 S. C. R. 717.	Judgment affirmed.
O'Toole v. Wallace (4 R. & G. 357).	S. C. Dig. 713.	Judgment reversed.
Patch v. Pitman (19 N. S. Rep. 298).	S. C. Dig. 389.	Judgment affirmed.
Peers v. Elliott (23 N. S. Rep. 276).	21 S. C. R. 19.	Judgment affirmed.
Peoples' Bank of Halifax v. Johnson (23 N. S. Rep. 302).	20 S. C. R. 541.	Judgment affirmed.
Pictou Railway Damages, in re (1 R. & G. 448).	S. C. Dig. 423 sub. nom. Hockin v. Halifax & C. B. Ry. & Coal Co.	Appeal quashed ; judgment not final.
Power v. Meagher (21 N. S. Rep. 184).	17 S. C. R. 287.	Judgment reversed.
Precedence of Ritchie, Q.C., in re (2 R. & C. 450).	3 S. C. R. 575 sub nom. Lenoir v. Ritchie.	Judgment affirmed.
Putnam v. Hardman (22 N. S. Rep. 456).	18 S. C. R. 714.	Judgment reversed.
Queen, The v. Chesley (6 R. & G. 313).	16 S. C. R. 306.	Judgment reversed.
Queen, The, v. Cunningham (6 R. & G. 31).	S. C. Dig. 194.	Judgment reversed.
Queen, The, v. Preeper (22 N. S. R. 174).	15 S. C. R. 401.	Judgment affirmed.
Queen, The, v. Town Council of Dartmouth (1 R. & G. 402).	9 S. C. R. 509.	Judgment affirmed.
(5 R. & G. 311).	S. C. Dig. 515.	Judgment that demurrer would lie affirmed.
Read v. County of Cape Breton (19 N. S. 260).	14 S. C. R. 8 sub nom. Crewe-Read v. Cape Breton.	Judgment reversed.
Ritchie v. Diocesan Synod of Nova Scotia (21 N. S. Rep. 309).	18 S. C. R. 705.	Judgment affirmed.
Robertson v. Pugh (20 N. S. Rep. 15).	15 S. C. R. 706.	Judgment affirmed.
Ross v. Hunter (2 R. & G. 44).	7 S. C. R. 289.	Judgment reversed.
Royal Canadian Ins. Co. v. Smith (5 R. & G. 322).	S. C. Dig. 385.	Judgment reversed.
Rumsey v. Merchants' Marine Ins. Co. (4 R. & G. 220).	9 S. C. R. 577.	Judgment affirmed.

CASE.	REPORT ON APPEAL.	RESULT OF APPEAL.
Seaman v. West (5 R. & G. 207).	S. C. Dig. 388.	Judgment affirmed.
Shanly v. Fitzrandolph (2 R. & G. 199).	S. C. Dig. 279.	Judgment affirmed.
Shelburne, Municipality of, v. Marshall (19 N. S. Rep. 171).	14 S. C. R. 737.	Judgment affirmed.
Silver v. Dominion Telegraph Co. (2 R. & G. 17).	10 S. C. R. 238.	Judgment reversed.
Smith v. McLean (24 N. S. Rep. 127).	21 S. C. R. 355.	Judgment reversed.
Smyth v. McDougall (1 R. & C. 371).	1 S. C. R. 114.	Judgment reversed.
Souther v. Wallace (2 R. & C. 548).	2 S. C. R. 598.	Judgment reversed.
(20 N. S. Rep. 509).	16 S. C. R. 717.	Judgment affirmed.
Spinney v. Ocean Mutual Marine Ins. Co. (21 N. S. Rep. 244).	17 S. C. R. 326.	Judgment affirmed.
Steel Co. of Canada, *in re* (5 R. & G. 17, 49, 141).	10 S. C. R. 312 *sub nom.* Merchants' Bank of Halifax v. Gillespie.	Judgment reversed.
Stuart v. Mott (23 N. S. Rep. 524). (24 N. S. Rep. 526).	14 S. C. R. 734.	Judgment affirmed. Stands for judgment.
Sword v. Sydney & Louisburg Coal & Ry. Co. (23 N. S. Rep. 214).	21 S. O. R. 152.	Judgment affirmed.
Tracey v. Young (5 R. & G. 381).	S. C. Dig. 147.	Judgment affirmed.
Troop v. Merchants' Marine Insurance Co. (6 R. & G. 323).	13 S. C. R. 506.	Judgment reversed.
Trustees of School Section 16, *in re* (2 R. & C. 328).	2 S. C. R. 690 *sub nom.* Pictou School Trustees v. Cameron.	Judgment reversed.
Union Bank of Halifax v. Whitman (20 N. S. Rep. 194).	16 S. C. R. 410.	Judgment affirmed.
Walker v. The City of Halifax (4 R. & G. 371).	S. C. Dig. 175.	Judgment affirmed.
Wallace v. Bossom (2 R. & C. 419).	2 S. C. R. 488.	Judgment reversed.
Watson v. Municipality of Colchester (6 R. & G. 549).	S. C. Dig. 175.	Judgment affirmed.
Webber v. Cogswell (2 R. & C. 47).	2 S. C. R. 15.	Judgment affirmed.
Webster v. Mutual Relief Soc. of Nova Scotia (20 N. S. Rep. 347).	16 S. C. R. 718.	Judgment affirmed.
Williston v. Lawson (22 N. S. Rep. 521).	19 S. C. R. 673.	Judgment affirmed.
Woodworth v. Troop (2 R. & C. 84).	2 S. C. R. 158 *sub nom.* Landers v. Woodsworth.	Judgment affirmed.
Wyman y. Imperial Ins. Co. (20 N. S. Rep. 487).	16 S. C. R. 715.	Judgment reversed.
York v. Canada Atlantic S. S. Co. (24 N. S. Rep. 436).	22 S. C. R. 167.	Judgment affirmed.

CASES IN THE COURTS OF NEW BRUNSWICK CARRIED TO THE PRIVY COUNCIL.

Case.	Report on Appeal.	Result of Appeal.
Arklow, The. Emery v. Cichero.	9 App. Cas. 136, 53 L. J. 9; 50 L. T. 305.	Judgment reversed.
Brookfield v. St. Andrews & Quebec Ry. Co. (N. B. Dig. 1231).	13 Moo. P. C. 510.	Judgment varied.
Bank of New Brunswick v. McLeod.	Beauchamp Dig. P. C. Cases 104.	Leave to appeal refused.
Dow v. Black.	L. R. 6 P. C. 272; 44 L. J. 52; 32 L. T. 274; 23 W. R. 637.	Judgment reversed.
McKay v. Commercial Bank (1 Pugs. 1).	L. R. 5 P. C. 394; 43 L. J. 31; 30 L. T. 180; 22 W. R. 473.	Judgment reversed.
Renaud, Ex parte (1 Pugs. 273).	None.	Judgment affirmed.
Ruggles v. Greene.	21 Can. Gaz. 415.	Judgment affirmed.
Russell v. The Queen.	7 App. Cas. 829; 51 L. J. 77; 46 L. T. 899.	Judgment affirmed.
Wickham v. New Brunswick & Canada Ry. Co. (6 All. 175.	L. R. 1 P. C. 64; 3 Moo. N. S. 416; 35 L. J. 6; 12 Jur. N. S. 34; 14 L. T. 311; 14 W. R. 251.	Judgment affirmed.

CASES IN THE NEW BRUNSWICK COURTS CARRIED TO THE SUPREME COURT OF CANADA.

CASE.	REPORT ON APPEAL.	RESULT OF APPEAL.
Albert Mining Co. v. Spurr (22 N. B. Rep. 346).	9 S. C. R. 35.	Judgment reversed.
Almon v. Lewin (4 P. & B. 284).	5 S. C. R. 514.	Judgment reversed.
Anderson v. Fawcett (24 N. B. Rep. 313) 3 P. & B. 34.	S. C. Dig. 8.	Judgment reversed.
Ayr American Plough Co. v. Wallace (30 N. B. Rep. 429).	21 S. C. R. 256.	Judgment affirmed.
Baird, Ex parte. In re Ellis (27 N. B. Rep. 99).	16 S. C. R. 147.	Appeal quashed as being premature.
Barss v. Merchants' Marine Ins. Co. (26 N. B. Rep. 339).	15 S. C. R. 185.	Judgment affirmed.
Burns v. Cassels (26 N. B. Rep. 20) 25 N. B. Rep. 13.	14 S. C. R. 256.	Judgment affirmed.
Busby v. Winchester (27 N. B. Rep. 231).	16 S. C. R. 336.	Judgment affirmed.
Byrne v. Arnold (24 N. B. Rep. 161).	S. C. Dig. 107.	Judgment affirmed.
Cameron v. Domville (1 P. & B. 647).	S. C. Dig. 421.	Appeal from rule for new trial quashed.
Chapman v. Delaware Mutual Ins. Co. (23 N. B. Rep. 121).	S. C. Dig. 387.	Judgment reversed.
Chapman v. Providence Washington Ins. Co. (23 N. B. Rep. 105).	S. C. Dig. 386.	Judgment affirmed.
Christie v. City of St. John (30 N. B. Rep. 492) 29 N. B. Rep. 311.	21 S. C. R. 1.	Judgment affirmed.
Clarke v. Scottish Imperial Ins. Co. (2 P. & B. 240).	4 S. C. R. 192.	Judgment reversed.
Cleveland, in re, (29 N. B. Rep. 70).	19 S. C. R. 78 sub nom. Lamb v. Cleveland.	Judgment affirmed.
Close v. Temple (4 P. & B. 234).	S. C. Dig. 765.	Judgment reversed.
Collins v. Everitt (2 P. & B. 469).	S. C. Dig. 210.	Judgment affirmed.
Commeau v. Burns [Gloucester Election] (22 N. B. Rep. 573).	8 S. C. R. 204.	Appeal quashed.
Connely v. Guardian Assur. Co. (30 N. B. Rep. 316).	20 S. C. R. 208.	Judgment affirmed.
Danaher, Ex parte, (27 N. B. Rep. 554).	17 S. C. R. 44 sub nom. Danaher v. Peters.	Judgment affirmed.
Driscoll v. Millville Mutual Ins. Co. (23 N. B. Rep. 160).	11 S. C. R. 183.	Judgment reversed.
Edwards v. Mayor, etc., of St. John (22 N. B. Rep. 297).	S. C. Dig. 48.	Judgment reversed.

CASE.	REPORT ON APPEAL.	RESULT OF APPEAL.
Elliott v. Flanagan (25 N. B. Rep. 154).	12 S. C. R. 435.	Judgment affirmed
Ellis v. Power (4 P. & B. 40).	6 S. C. R. 1.	Judgment reversed.
Fairweather, *Ex parte*, (30 N. B. Rep. 531).	Peters v. City of St. John, 21 S. C. R. 674.	Judgment reversed.
Ferguson v. Troop (28 N. B. Rep. 301) 25 N. B. Rep. 440).	17 S. C. R. 527.	Judgment reversed.
Gerow v. Providence Washington Ins. Co. (28 N. B. Rep. 435).	17 S. C. R. 387.	Judgment affirmed.
Gerow v. Royal Canadian Ins. Co. (27 N. B. Rep. 513).	16 S. C. R. 524.	Judgment affirmed.
Gilbert v. McDonald (28 N. B. Rep. 102).	16 S. C. R. 700.	Judgment affirmed.
Gilchrist v. Dominion Telegraph Co. (4 P. & B. 241) 3 P. & B. 553.	S. C. Dig. 844.	Judgment affirmed.
Gleeson v. Domville (3 P. & B. 77.	S. C. Dig. 343.	Judgment reversed.
Griffiths v. Town of Portland (23 N. B. Rep. 559).	11 S. C. R. 333.	Judgment reversed.
Halifax Banking Co. v. Smith (29 N. B. Rep. 462).	18 S. C. R. 710.	Judgment reversed.
Hall v. McFadden (21 N. B. Rep. 586) 3 P. & B. 340.	S. C. Dig. 723.	Judgment affirmed,
Harris v. Greene (25 N. B. Rep. 451.	16 S. C. R. 714.	Judgment reversed.
Hutchinson v. Trustees of St. John Y. M. C. A. (2 P. & B. 523).	S. C. Dig. 210.	Judgment affirmed.
Jonas v. Gilbert (4 P. & P. 61, 64).	5 S. C. R. 356.	Judgment reversed.
Jones v. DeWolf (23 N. B. Rep. 356).	S. C. Dig. 767.	Judgment affirmed.
Jones v. Tuck (23 N. B. Rep. 447).	11 S. C. R. 197.	Judgment reversed.
Jordan v. Great Western Ins. Co. (24 N. B. Rep. 421).	14 S. C. R. 734.	Judgment reversed.
Lawless, *Ex parte*, (2 P. & B. 520).	3 S. C. R. 117 *sub nom.* Lawless v. Sullivan ; rev. by Pr. Coun. 6 App. Cas. 373.	Judgment affirmed, but reversed on further appeal.
Lewin, *Ex parte*, (23 N. B. Rep. 591).	11 S. C. R. 484.	Judgment reversed.
Lockhart, Executor, etc., v. Ray (4 P. & B. 120).	6 S. C. R. 308 *sub nom.* Ray v. Annual Conference of N. B.	Judgment affirmed.
Maritime Bank, *in re* Troop's Case (27 N. B. Rep. 295).	16 S. C. R. 456.	Judgment reversed.
Moran v. Taylor (24 N. B. Rep. 39).	11 S. C. R. 347.	Judgment reversed.
McDonald v. Mayor, etc., of St. John (25 N. B. Rep. 318) 24 N. B. Rep. 370.	14 S. C. R. 1.	Judgment affirmed.
McFee v. Mowat (3 P. & B. 252).	5 S. C. R. 66.	Judgment affirmed.
McGibee v. Phœnix Ins. Co. (28 N. B. Rep. 45).	18 S. C. R. 61.	New trial ordered.
McKean v. Jones (29 N. B. Rep. 340).	19 S. C. R. 489.	Judgment affirmed.

CASE.	REPORT ON APPEAL.	RESULT OF APPEAL.
McLellan v. North British & Mercantile Ins. Co. (30 N. B. Rep. 263).	21 S. C. R. 288.	Judgment affirmed.
McMillan v. South-West Boom Co. (1 P. & B. 715).	3 S. C. R. 700.	Judgment affirmed.
McMillan v. Walker (21 N. B. Rep. 31).	6 S. C. R. 241.	Judgment affirmed.
McSorley v. Mayor, etc., of St. John (4 P. & B. 479).	6 S. C. R. 531.	Judgment reversed.
New Brunswick Ry. Co. v. McLeod (1 P. & B. 257).	5 S. C. R. 281.	Judgment affirmed by equal division.
Nicholson v. Temple (4 P. & B. 248).	S. C. Dig. 114.	Judgment affirmed.
O'Brien v. O'Brien (27 N. B. Rep. 145.	S. C. Dig. 297.	Judgment affirmed.
Parker v. White (27 N. B. Rep. 442).	16 S. C. R. 699.	Appeal quashed ; no cause before Court.
Pattison v. Mayor, etc., of St. John (2 P. & B. 636).	S. C. Dig. 173.	Judgment reversed.
People's National Bank of Charleston v. Stewart (3 P. & B. 268).	S. C. Dig. 81.	Judgment affirmed.
Peters v. Hamilton (3 P. & B. 284).	S. C. Dig. 763.	Judgment reversed.
Provincial Government of N. B. v. Maritime Bank (27 N. B. Rep. 379).	20 S. C. R. 695 ; aff. by Pr. Coun. [1892] A. C. 437.	Judgment reversed in part.
Queen, The, v. Ellis. *Ex parte* Baird (28 N. B. Rep. 497).	22 S. C. R. 7.	Appeal in criminal case quashed.
Queen, The, v. Maritime Bank, (27 N. B. Rep. 357).	17 S. C. R. 657.	Judgment reversed in part.
Queen, The, v. Mayor, etc., of Fredericton (3 P. & B. 139).	3 S. C. R. 505.	Judgment reversed.
Queen, The, v. McFarlance (27 N. B. Rep. 529).	16 S. C. R. 393.	Judgment affirmed.
Queen, The, v. Theal (21 N. B. Rep. 449).	7 S. C. R. 397.	Judgment affirmed.
Rand, *Ex parte* (24 N. B. Rep. 374).	11 S. C. R. 312 *sub nom.* Chapman v. Rand.	Judgment reversed.
Richardson v. Vaughan (28 N. B. Rep. 364) 24 N. B. Rep. 75.	{ 17 S. C. R. 703. 21 S. C. R. 359.	Appeal quashed for want of notice. Judgment affirmed.
Ring v. Pugsley (2 P. & B. 303).	S. C. Dig. 241.	Judgment reversed.
Ritchie v. Snowball (26 N. B. Rep. 258).	14 S. C. R. 741.	Judgment reversed.
Robinson v. New Brunswick Ry. Co. (23 N. B. Rep. 323).	11 S. C. R. 688.	Judgment reversed.
Scammell v. James (28 N. B. Rep. 278).	16 S. C. R. 593.	Appeal quashed ; proper parties not before Court.
Schofield v. Carvill (21 N. B. Rep. 558).	9 S. C. R. 370.	Judgment affirmed.
Shireff v. Muirhead (25 N. B. Rep. 196).	14 S. C. R. 735.	Judgment affirmed.
Simonds v. Chesley (30 N. B. Rep. 303).	20 S. C. R. 174.	Judgment affirmed.
Steadman v. Venning (22 N. B. Rep. 639).	9 S. C. R. 206.	Judgment reversed.
Stephenson v. Fraser (24 N. B. Rep. 482).	S. C. Dig. 575.	Judgment reversed.
Stephenson v. Miller (27 N. B. Rep. 42).	16 S. C. R. 722.	Judgment affirmed.

CASE.	REPORT ON APPEAL.	RESULT OF APPEAL.
Stewart v. Snowball (3 P. & B. 597).	S. C. Dig. 570.	Judgment reversed.
St. John, Mayor, etc., of v. Sears (28 N. B. Rep. 1).	18 S. C. R. 702.	Judgment affirmed.
Swim v. Sheriff (4 P. & B. 25).	S. C. Dig. 142.	Judgment affirmed.
Swinny v. Rodburn (27 N. B. Rep. 175).	16 S. C. R. 297.	Judgment affirmed.
Tufts v. Chapman (22 N. B. Rep. 195).	8 S. C. R. 543.	Judgment affirmed.
Vanwart v. New Brunswick Ry. Co. (27 N. B. Rep. 59).	17 S. C. R. 35.	Judgment reversed.
Vaughan v. Roberts (23 N. B. Rep. 343).	11 S. C. R. 273.	Judgment reversed.
Vernon v. Oliver (23 N. B. Rep. 392).	11 S. C. R. 156.	Judgment reversed.
Vye v. Alexander (28 N. B. Rep. 89).	16 S. C. R. 501.	Judgment affirmed.
Waterbury v. Dewe (3 P. & B. 225).	6 S. C. R. 143.	Judgment reversed.
Waterous Co. v. Morrow (2 P. & B. 11).	S. C. Dig. 138.	Judgment reversed.
Weldon v. Vaughan (2 P. & B. 70).	5 S. C. R. 35.	Judgment reversed.
White v. Miller (27 N. B. Rep. 143).	16 S. C. R. 445.	Judgment reversed:
Williams v. City of Portland (29 N. B. Rep. 1).	19 S. C. R. 159.	Judgment affirmed.
Wood v. Vaughan (28 N. B. Rep. 472).	18 S. C. R. 703.	Judgment affirmed.

CASES FROM THE COURTS OF MANITOBA CARRIED TO THE PRIVY COUNCIL.

CASE.	REPORT ON APPEAL.	RESULT OF APPEAL.
Logan v. City of Winnipeg (8 Man. L. R. 3).	[1892] A. C. 445; 61 L. J. 58; 67 L. T. 429.	Judgment affirmed.
The Queen v. Riel (2 Man. L. R. 321) 2 Man. L. R. 302).	10 App. Cas. 675; 55 L. J. 28 ; 54 L. T. 339.	Leave to appeal refused.
Winnipeg Street Ry. Co. v. Winnipeg Elec. Ry. Co.	22 Can. Gaz. 584.	Stands for Judgment,

CASES FROM THE MANITOBA COURTS CARRIED TO THE SUPREME COURT OF CANADA.

CASE.	REPORT ON APPEAL.	RESULT OF APPEAL.
Ashdown v. Manitoba Free Press Co. (6 Man. L. R. 578).	20 S. C. R. 43.	Judgment affirmed.
Atty.-Gen. Canada v. Fonseca (5 Man. L. R. 173).	17 S. C. R. 612.	Judgment reversed.
Barrett v. City of Winnipeg (7 Man. L. R. 273).	19 S. C. R. 374; rev. by Pr. Coun. [1892] A. C. 445.	Judgment reversed, but restored on further appeal.
Bernardine v. Municipality of North Dufferin (6 Man. L. R. 88).	19 S. C. R. 581.	Judgment reversed.
Canadian Pacific Ry. Co. v. Municipality of Cornwallis (7 Man. L. R. 1).	19 S. C. R. 702.	Judgment affirmed.
Dederick v. Ashdown (4 Man. L. R. 139).	15 S. C. R. 227.	Judgment reversed.
Federal Bank of Canada v. Canadian Bank of Commerce (2 Man. L. R. 257).	13 S. C. R. 384.	Judgment affirmed.
Hutchinson v. Calder (1 Man. L. R. 46) 1 Man. L. R. 17.	S. C. Dig. 785.	Judgment affirmed.

CASE.	REPORT ON APPEAL.	RESULT OF APPEAL.
Lisgar Election Case [Collins v. Ross] (7 Man. L. R. 581).	20 S. C. R. 1.	Judgment reversed in part.
London & Canadian Loan Co. v. Municipality of Morris (7 Man. L. R. 128).	19 S. C. R. 434.	Appeal quashed ; judgment not final.
Martin v. Manitoba Free Press Co. (8 Man. L. R. 50) 7 Man. L. R. 413.	21 S. C. R. 518.	Judgment affirmed.
Morden v. Municipality South Dufferin (6 Man. L. R. 515).	19 S. C. R. 204.	Judgment reversed.
McMillan v. Byers (4 Man. L. R. 76) 3 Man. L. R. 361.	15 S. C. R. 194.	Judgment reversed.
Ontario Bank v. McMicken (7 Man. L. R. 203).	20 S. C. R. 548.	Judgment affirmed.
Reg. v. Nevins (5 Man. L. R. 153).	S. C. Dig. 427.	Appeal quashed ; case not originating in Superior Court.
Rolston v. Red River Bridge Co. (1 Man. L. R. 235).	S. C. Dig. 564.	Judgment affirmed.
Ryan v. Whelan (6 Man. L. R. 565).	20 S. C. R. 65.	Judgment affirmed.
Shaw v. Canadian Pacific Ry. Co. (5 Man. L. R. 334) 5 Man. L. R. 198.	16 S. C. R. 703.	Appeal from judgment on demurrer quashed.
Stephen's v. McArthur (6 Man. L. R. 496).	19 S. C. R. 446.	Judgment reversed.
Union Bank v. Bulmer, 2 Man. L. R. 380.	S. C. Dig. 88.	Judgment reversed.
Wright v. City of Winnipeg (4 Man. L. R. 46).	13 S. C. R. 441.	Leave to extend time to appeal refused.

CASES FROM THE COURTS OF BRITISH COLUM-BIA CARRIED TO THE SUPREME COURT OF CANADA.

CASE.	REPORT ON APPEAL.	RESULT OF APPEAL.
Edmonds v. Tiernan (2 B. C. R. 82).	21 S. C. R. 406.	Judgment affirmed.
Foley v. Webster (2 B. C. R. 137).	21 S. C. R. 580.	Judgment affirmed.
Harper v. Harper (2 B. C. R. 15).	21 S. C. R. 273 *sub nom.* Cameron v. Harper.	Judgment affirmed.
Sea v. McLean (2 B. C. L. R. 67).	14 S. C. R. 632.	Judgment reversed.

CASES FROM THE COURTS OF PRINCE EDWARD ISLAND CARRIED TO THE PRIVY COUNCIL.

CASE.	REPORT ON APPEAL.	RESULT OF APPEAL.
Cambridge, *in re.*	3 Moo. P. C. 175.	Leave to appeal refused ; appeal lay only from Executive Council.
Monkton, *in re.*	1 Moo. P. C. 455.	Judgment reversed.

CASES IN THE COURTS OF PRINCE EDWARD ISLAND CARRIED TO THE SUPREME COURT OF CANADA.

CASE.	REPORT ON APPEAL.	RESULT OF APPEAL.
Holman v. Green (2 P. E. I. Rep. 329).	6 S. C. R. 707.	Judgment affirmed.
Kelly v. Sulivan (2 P. E. I. Rep. 34).	1 S. C. R. 1.	Judgment reversed.

CASES IN THE COURTS OF THE NORTH-WEST TERRITORIES CARRIED TO THE SUPREME COURT OF CANADA.

CASE.	REPORT ON APPEAL.	RESULT OF APPEAL.
Angus v. Calgary School Board (N.-W. T. Rep. [Pt. I.] 40).	16 S. C. R. 716.	Appeal quashed : case not originating in Superior Court.
Emerson v. Bannerman (1 N.-W. T. Rep. [Pt. II.] 35).	19 S. C. R. 1.	Judgment affirmed.
Ferguson v. Fairchild (1 N.-W. T. Rep. [Pt. III.] 41).	21 S. C. R. 484.	Judgment affirmed.
Moore v. Martin (1 N.-W. T. Rep. [Pt. II] 48).	18 S. C. R. 634.	Appeal quashed ; judgment not final.
Quirk v. Thompson (1 N.-W. T. Rep. [Pt. I.] 88).	18 S. C. R. 695.	Judgment affirmed.

www.ingramcontent.com/pod-product-compliance
Lightning Source LLC
Chambersburg PA
CBHW031456270326
41930CB00007B/1022